THE JOY OF THE GOSPEL

POPE FRANCIS

DynamicCatholic.com
Be Bold. Be Catholic.®

APOSTOLIC EXHORTATION

EVANGELII GAUDIUM

OF THE HOLY FATHER

FRANCIS

TO THE BISHOPS, CLERGY,
CONSECRATED PERSONS
AND THE LAY FAITHFUL
ON THE PROCLAMATION OF THE GOSPEL
IN TODAY'S WORLD

THE JOY OF THE GOSPEL

ISBN (Soft Cover): 978-1-937509-82-8
ISBN (Hard Cover): 978-1-937509-86-6

Design by Jenny Miller and Shawna Powell

For more information on this title
and other books and CDs available through
the Dynamic Catholic Book Program, please visit:
www.DynamicCatholic.com

The Dynamic Catholic Institute
5081 Olympic Blvd • Erlanger • Kentucky • 41018
Phone: 1-859-980-7900
Email: info@DynamicCatholic.com

TABLE OF CONTENTS

1. The joy of the gospel fills the hearts and lives of all who encounter Jesus. Those who accept his offer of salvation are set free from sin, sorrow, inner emptiness and loneliness. With Christ joy is constantly born anew. In this Exhortation I wish to encourage the Christian faithful to embark upon a new chapter of evangelization marked by this joy, while pointing out new paths for the Church's journey in years to come.

I. A JOY EVER NEW, A JOY WHICH IS SHARED

2. The great danger in today's world, pervaded as it is by consumerism, is the desolation and anguish born of a complacent yet covetous heart, the feverish pursuit of frivolous pleasures, and a blunted conscience. Whenever our interior life becomes caught up in its own interests and concerns, there is no longer room for others, no place for the poor. God's voice is no longer heard, the quiet joy of his love is no longer felt, and the desire to do good fades. This is a very real danger for believers too. Many fall prey to it, and end up resentful, angry and listless. That is no way to live a dignified and fulfilled life; it is not God's will for us, nor is it the life in the Spirit which has its source in the heart of the risen Christ.

3. I invite all Christians, everywhere, at this very moment, to a renewed personal encounter with Jesus Christ, or at least an openness to letting him encounter them; I ask all

of you to do this unfailingly each day. No one should think that this invitation is not meant for him or her, since "no one is excluded from the joy brought by the Lord".[1] The Lord does not disappoint those who take this risk; whenever we take a step towards Jesus, we come to realize that he is already there, waiting for us with open arms. Now is the time to say to Jesus: "Lord, I have let myself be deceived; in a thousand ways I have shunned your love, yet here I am once more, to renew my covenant with you. I need you. Save me once again, Lord, take me once more into your redeeming embrace". How good it feels to come back to him whenever we are lost! Let me say this once more: God never tires of forgiving us; we are the ones who tire of seeking his mercy. Christ, who told us to forgive one another "seventy times seven" (Mt 18:22) has given us his example: he has forgiven us seventy times seven. Time and time again he bears us on his shoulders. No one can strip us of the dignity bestowed upon us by this boundless and unfailing love. With a tenderness which never disappoints, but is always capable of restoring our joy, he makes it possible for us to lift up our heads and to start anew. Let us not flee from the resurrection of Jesus, let us never give up, come what will. May nothing inspire more than his life, which impels us onwards!

---

1. Paul VI, Apostolic Exhortation *Gaudete in Domino* (9 May 1975), 22: AAS 67 (1975), 297.

4. The books of the Old Testament predicted that the joy of salvation would abound in messianic times. The prophet Isaiah exultantly salutes the awaited Messiah: "You have multiplied the nation, you have increased its joy" (9:3). He exhorts those who dwell on Zion to go forth to meet him with song: "Shout aloud and sing for joy!" (12:6). The prophet tells those who have already seen him from afar to bring the message to others: "Get you up to a high mountain, O herald of good tidings to Zion; lift up your voice with strength, O herald of good tidings to Jerusalem" (40:9). All creation shares in the joy of salvation: "Sing for joy, O heavens, and exult, O earth! Break forth, O mountains, into singing! For the Lord has comforted his people, and will have compassion on his suffering ones" (49:13).

Zechariah, looking to the day of the Lord, invites the people to acclaim the king who comes "humble and riding on a donkey": "Rejoice greatly, O daughter Zion! Shout aloud, O daughter Jerusalem! Lo, your king comes to you; triumphant and victorious is he" (9:9).

Perhaps the most exciting invitation is that of the prophet Zephaniah, who presents God with his people in the midst of a celebration overflowing with the joy of salvation. I find it thrilling to reread this text: "The Lord, your God is in your midst, a warrior who gives you the victory; he will rejoice over you with gladness, he will renew you in his love; he will exult over you with loud singing, as on a day of festival" (3:17).

This is the joy which we experience daily, amid the little things of life, as a response to the loving invitation of God our Father: "My child, treat yourself well, according to your means... Do not deprive yourself of the day's enjoyment" (Sir 14:11, 14). What tender paternal love echoes in these words!

5. The Gospel, radiant with the glory of Christ's cross, constantly invites us to rejoice. A few examples will suffice. "Rejoice!" is the angel's greeting to Mary (Lk 1:28). Mary's visit to Elizabeth makes John leap for joy in his mother's womb (cf. Lk 1:41). In her song of praise, Mary proclaims: "My spirit rejoices in God my Saviour" (Lk 1:47). When Jesus begins his ministry, John cries out: "For this reason, my joy has been fulfilled" (Jn 3:29). Jesus himself "rejoiced in the Holy Spirit" (Lk 10:21). His message brings us joy: "I have said these things to you, so that my joy may be in you, and that your joy may be complete" (Jn 15:11). Our Christian joy drinks of the wellspring of his brimming heart. He promises his disciples: "You will be sorrowful, but your sorrow will turn into joy" (Jn 16:20). He then goes on to say: "But I will see you again and your hearts will rejoice, and no one will take your joy from you" (Jn 16:22). The disciples "rejoiced" (Jn 20:20) at the sight of the risen Christ. In the Acts of the Apostles we read that the first Christians "ate their food with glad and generous hearts" (2:46). Wherever the disciples went, "there was great joy" (8:8); even amid persecution they continued to be "filled with joy" (13:52). The newly baptized eunuch "went on his way rejoicing" (8:39), while Paul's jailer "and his entire household rejoiced that he had become a believer

in God" (16:34). Why should we not also enter into this great stream of joy?

6. There are Christians whose lives seem like Lent without Easter. I realize of course that joy is not expressed the same way at all times in life, especially at moments of great difficulty. Joy adapts and changes, but it always endures, even as a flicker of light born of our personal certainty that, when everything is said and done, we are infinitely loved. I understand the grief of people who have to endure great suffering, yet slowly but surely we all have to let the joy of faith slowly revive as a quiet yet firm trust, even amid the greatest distress: "My soul is bereft of peace; I have forgotten what happiness is... But this I call to mind, and therefore I have hope: the steadfast love of the Lord never ceases, his mercies never come to an end; they are new every morning. Great is your faithfulness... It is good that one should wait quietly for the salvation of the Lord" (Lam 3:17, 21-23, 26).

7. Sometimes we are tempted to find excuses and complain, acting as if we could only be happy if a thousand conditions were met. To some extent this is because our "technological society has succeeded in multiplying occasions of pleasure, yet has found it very difficult to engender joy".[2] I can say that the most beautiful and natural expressions of joy which I have seen in my life were in

---

2. Ibid. 8: AAS 67 (1975), 292.

poor people who had little to hold on to. I also think of the real joy shown by others who, even amid pressing professional obligations, were able to preserve, in detachment and simplicity, a heart full of faith. In their own way, all these instances of joy flow from the infinite love of God, who has revealed himself to us in Jesus Christ. I never tire of repeating those words of Benedict XVI which take us to the very heart of the Gospel: "Being a Christian is not the result of an ethical choice or a lofty idea, but the encounter with an event, a person, which gives life a new horizon and a decisive direction".[3]

8. Thanks solely to this encounter – or renewed encounter – with God's love, which blossoms into an enriching friendship, we are liberated from our narrowness and self-absorption. We become fully human when we become more than human, when we let God bring us beyond ourselves in order to attain the fullest truth of our being. Here we find the source and inspiration of all our efforts at evangelization. For if we have received the love which restores meaning to our lives, how can we fail to share that love with others?

---

3. Encyclical Letter *Deus Caritas Est* (25 December 2005), 1: AAS 98 (2006), 217.

II. THE **DELIGHTFUL** AND **COMFORTING** JOY OF EVANGELIZING

9. Goodness always tends to spread. Every authentic experience of truth and goodness seeks by its very nature to grow within us, and any person who has experienced a profound liberation becomes more sensitive to the needs of others. As it expands, goodness takes root and develops. If we wish to lead a dignified and fulfilling life, we have to reach out to others and seek their good. In this regard, several sayings of Saint Paul will not surprise us: "The love of Christ urges us on" (2 Cor 5:14); "Woe to me if I do not proclaim the Gospel" (1 Cor 9:16).

10. The Gospel offers us the chance to live life on a higher plane, but with no less intensity: "Life grows by being given away, and it weakens in isolation and comfort. Indeed, those who enjoy life most are those who leave security on the shore and become excited by the mission of communicating life to others".[4] When the Church summons Christians to take up the task of evangelization, she is simply pointing to the source of authentic personal fulfilment. For "here we discover a profound law of reality: that life is attained and matures in the measure that it is offered up in order to give life to others. This is certainly what mission

---

4. Fifth General Conference of the Latin American and Caribbean Bishops, *Aparecida Document*, 29 June 2007, 360.

means".[5] Consequently, an evangelizer must never look like someone who has just come back from a funeral! Let us recover and deepen our enthusiasm, that "delightful and comforting joy of evangelizing, even when it is in tears that we must sow... And may the world of our time, which is searching, sometimes with anguish, sometimes with hope, be enabled to receive the good news not from evangelizers who are dejected, discouraged, impatient or anxious, but from ministers of the Gospel whose lives glow with fervour, who have first received the joy of Christ".[6]

Eternal Newness

11. A renewal of preaching can offer believers, as well as the lukewarm and the non-practising, new joy in the faith and fruitfulness in the work of evangelization. The heart of its message will always be the same: the God who revealed his immense love in the crucified and risen Christ. God constantly renews his faithful ones, whatever their age: "They shall mount up with wings like eagles, they shall run and not be weary, they shall walk and not be faint" (Is 40:31). Christ is the "eternal Gospel" (Rev 14:6); he "is the same yesterday and today and forever" (Heb 13:8), yet his riches and beauty are inexhaustible. He is for ever young and a constant source of newness. The Church never fails

---

5. Ibid.

6. Paul VI, Apostolic Exhortation *Evangelii Nuntiandi* (8 December 1975), 80: AAS 68 (1976), 75.

to be amazed at "the depth of the riches and wisdom and knowledge of God" (Rom 11:33). Saint John of the Cross says that "the thicket of God's wisdom and knowledge is so deep and so broad that the soul, however much it has come to know of it, can always penetrate deeper within it".[7] Or as Saint Irenaeus writes: "By his coming, Christ brought with him all newness".[8] With this newness he is always able to renew our lives and our communities, and even if the Christian message has known periods of darkness and ecclesial weakness, it will never grow old. Jesus can also break through the dull categories with which we would enclose him and he constantly amazes us by his divine creativity. Whenever we make the effort to return to the source and to recover the original freshness of the Gospel, new avenues arise, new paths of creativity open up, with different forms of expression, more eloquent signs and words with new meaning for today's world. Every form of authentic evangelization is always "new".

12. Though it is true that this mission demands great generosity on our part, it would be wrong to see it as a heroic individual undertaking, for it is first and foremost the Lord's work, surpassing anything which we can see and understand. Jesus is "the first and greatest evangelizer".[9]

---

7. *Spiritual Canticle*, 36, 10.

8. *Adversus Haereses*, IV, c. 34, n. 1: PG 7, pars prior, 1083: " Omnem novitatem attulit, semetipsum afferens".

9. Paul VI, Apostolic Exhortation *Evangelii Nuntiandi* (8 December 1975), 7: AAS 68 (1976), 9.

In every activity of evangelization, the primacy always belongs to God, who has called us to cooperate with him and who leads us on by the power of his Spirit. The real newness is the newness which God himself mysteriously brings about and inspires, provokes, guides and accompanies in a thousand ways. The life of the Church should always reveal clearly that God takes the initiative, that "he has loved us first" (1 Jn 4:19) and that he alone "gives the growth" (1 Cor 3:7). This conviction enables us to maintain a spirit of joy in the midst of a task so demanding and challenging that it engages our entire life. God asks everything of us, yet at the same time he offers everything to us.

13. Nor should we see the newness of this mission as entailing a kind of displacement or forgetfulness of the living history which surrounds us and carries us forward. Memory is a dimension of our faith which we might call "deuteronomic", not unlike the memory of Israel itself. Jesus leaves us the Eucharist as the Church's daily remembrance of, and deeper sharing in, the event of his Passover (cf. Lk 22:19). The joy of evangelizing always arises from grateful remembrance: it is a grace which we constantly need to implore. The apostles never forgot the moment when Jesus touched their hearts: "It was about four o'clock in the afternoon" (Jn 1:39). Together with Jesus, this remembrance makes present to us "a great cloud of witnesses" (Heb 12:1), some of whom, as believers, we recall with great joy: "Remember your leaders, those who spoke to you the word of God" (Heb 13:7). Some of them were ordinary people

who were close to us and introduced us to the life of faith: "I am reminded of your sincere faith, a faith that dwelt first in your grandmother Lois and your mother Eunice" (2 Tim 1:5). The believer is essentially "one who remembers".

III. THE NEW EVANGELIZATION FOR THE TRANSMISSION OF THE FAITH

14. Attentive to the promptings of the Holy Spirit who helps us together to read the signs of the times, the XIII Ordinary General Assembly of the Synod of Bishops gathered from 7-28 October 2012 to discuss the theme: The *New Evangelization for the Transmission of the Christian Faith.* The Synod reaffirmed that the new evangelization is a summons addressed to all and that it is carried out in three principal settings.[10]

15. In first place, we can mention the area of ordinary pastoral ministry, which is "animated by the fire of the Spirit, so as to inflame the hearts of the faithful who regularly take part in community worship and gather on the Lord's day to be nourished by his word and by the bread of eternal life".[11] In this category we can also include those members of faithful who preserve a deep and sincere faith, express-

---

10. Cf. *Propositio* 7.

11. Benedict XVI, Homily at Mass for the Conclusion of the Synod of Bishops (28 October 2012): AAS 104 (2102), 890.

ing it in different ways, but seldom taking part in worship. Ordinary pastoral ministry seeks to help believers to grow spiritually so that they can respond to God's love ever more fully in their lives.

A second area is that of *"the baptized whose lives do not reflect the demands of Baptism"*,[12] who lack a meaningful relationship to the Church and no longer experience the consolation born of faith. The Church, in her maternal concern, tries to help them experience a conversion which will restore the joy of faith to their hearts and inspire a commitment to the Gospel.

Lastly, we cannot forget that evangelization is first and foremost about preaching the Gospel to *those who do not know Jesus Christ or who have always rejected him*. Many of them are quietly seeking God, led by a yearning to see his face, even in countries of ancient Christian tradition. All of them have a right to receive the Gospel. Christians have the duty to proclaim the Gospel without excluding anyone. Instead of seeming to impose new obligations, they should appear as people who wish to share their joy, who point to a horizon of beauty and who invite others to a delicious banquet. It is not by proselytizing that the Church grows, but "by attraction".[13]

John Paul II asked us to recognize that "there must be no lessening of the impetus to preach the Gospel" to those

---

12. Ibid.

13. Benedict XVI, Homily at Mass for the Opening of the Fifth General Conference of the Latin American and Caribbean Bishops (13 May 2007), Aparecida, Brazil: AAS 99 (2007), 437.

who are far from Christ, "because this is the first task of the Church".[14] Indeed, "today missionary activity still represents the greatest challenge for the Church"[15] and "the missionary task must remain foremost".[16] What would happen if we were to take these words seriously? We would realize that missionary outreach is *paradigmatic for all the Church's activity*. Along these lines the Latin American bishops stated that we "cannot passively and calmly wait in our church buildings";[17] we need to move "from a pastoral ministry of mere conservation to a decidedly missionary pastoral ministry".[18] This task continues to be a source of immense joy for the Church: "Just so, I tell you, there will be more joy in heaven over one sinner who repents than ninety-nine righteous persons who need no repentance" (Lk 15:7).

The Scope and Limits of this Exhortation

16. I was happy to take up the request of the Fathers of the Synod to write this Exhortation.[19] In so doing, I am reaping the rich fruits of the Synod's labours. In addition,

---

14. Encyclical Letter, *Redemptoris Missio* (7 December 1990), 34: AAS 83 (1991), 280.

15. Ibid., 40: AAS 83 (1991), 287.

16. Ibid., 86: AAS 83 (1991), 333.

17. Fifth General Conference of the Latin American and Caribbean Bishops, *Aparecida Document*, 29 June 2007, 548.

18. Ibid., 370.

19. Cf. *Propositio* 1.

I have sought advice from a number of people and I intend to express my own concerns about this particular chapter of the Church's work of evangelization. Countless issues involving evangelization today might be discussed here, but I have chosen not to explore these many questions which call for further reflection and study. Nor do I believe that the papal magisterium should be expected to offer a definitive or complete word on every question which affects the Church and the world. It is not advisable for the Pope to take the place of local Bishops in the discernment of every issue which arises in their territory. In this sense, I am conscious of the need to promote a sound "decentralization".

17. Here I have chosen to present some guidelines which can encourage and guide the whole Church in a new phase of evangelization, one marked by enthusiasm and vitality. In this context, and on the basis of the teaching of the Dogmatic Constitution *Lumen Gentium*, I have decided, among other themes, to discuss at length the following questions:

a) The reform of the Church in her missionary outreach;
b) The temptations faced by pastoral workers;
c) The Church, understood as the entire People of God which evangelizes;
d) The homily and its preparation;
e) The inclusion of the poor in society;
f) Peace and dialogue within society;
g) The spiritual motivations for mission.

18. I have dealt extensively with these topics, with a detail which some may find excessive. But I have done so, not with the intention of providing an exhaustive treatise but simply as a way of showing their important practical implications for the Church's mission today. All of them help give shape to a definite style of evangelization which I ask you to adopt *in every activity which you undertake*. In this way, we can take up, amid our daily efforts, the biblical exhortation: "Rejoice in the Lord always; again I will say: Rejoice" (Phil 4:4).

CHAPTER ONE

THE CHURCH'S MISSIONARY TRANSFORMATION

19. Evangelization takes place in obedience to the missionary mandate of Jesus: "Go therefore and make disciples of all nations, baptizing them in the name of the Father and of the Son and of the Holy Spirit, teaching them to observe all that I have commanded you" (Mt 28:19-20). In these verses we see how the risen Christ sent his followers to preach the Gospel in every time and place, so that faith in him might spread to every corner of the earth.

I. A CHURCH WHICH GOES FORTH

20. The word of God constantly shows us how God challenges those who believe in him "to go forth". Abraham received the call to set out for a new land (cf. Gen 12:1-3). Moses heard God's call: "Go, I send you" (Ex 3:10) and led the people towards the promised land (cf. Ex 3:17). To

Jeremiah God says: "To all whom I send you, you shall go" (Jer 1:7). In our day Jesus' command to "go and make disciples" echoes in the changing scenarios and ever new challenges to the Church's mission of evangelization, and all of us are called to take part in this new missionary "going forth". Each Christian and every community must discern the path that the Lord points out, but all of us are asked to obey his call to go forth from our own comfort zone in order to reach all the "peripheries" in need of the light of the Gospel.

21. The Gospel joy which enlivens the community of disciples is a missionary joy. The seventy-two disciples felt it as they returned from their mission (cf. Lk 10:17). Jesus felt it when he rejoiced in the Holy Spirit and praised the Father for revealing himself to the poor and the little ones (cf. Lk 10:21). It was felt by the first converts who marvelled to hear the apostles preaching "in the native language of each" (Acts 2:6) on the day of Pentecost. This joy is a sign that the Gospel has been proclaimed and is bearing fruit. Yet the drive to go forth and give, to go out from ourselves, to keep pressing forward in our sowing of the good seed, remains ever present. The Lord says: "Let us go on to the next towns that I may preach there also, for that is why I came out" (Mk 1:38). Once the seed has been sown in one place, Jesus does not stay behind to explain things or to perform more signs; the Spirit moves him to go forth to other towns.

22. God's word is unpredictable in its power. The Gospel speaks of a seed which, once sown, grows by itself, even as the farmer sleeps (Mk 4:26-29). The Church has to accept this unruly freedom of the word, which accomplishes what it wills in ways that surpass our calculations and ways of thinking.

23. The Church's closeness to Jesus is part of a common journey; "communion and mission are profoundly interconnected".[20] In fidelity to the example of the Master, it is vitally important for the Church today to go forth and preach the Gospel to all: to all places, on all occasions, without hesitation, reluctance or fear. The joy of the Gospel is for all people: no one can be excluded. That is what the angel proclaimed to the shepherds in Bethlehem: "Be not afraid; for behold, I bring you good news of a great joy which will come to all the people (Lk 2:10). The Book of Revelation speaks of "an eternal Gospel to proclaim to those who dwell on earth, to every nation and tongue and tribe and people" (Rev 14:6).

Taking the First Step, Being Involved and Supportive, Bearing Fruit and Rejoicing

24. The Church which "goes forth" is a community of missionary disciples who take the first step, who are involved

---

20. John Paul II, Post-Synodal Apostolic Exhortation *Christifideles Laici* (30 December 1988), 32: AAS 81 (1989) 451.

and supportive, who bear fruit and rejoice. An evangelizing community knows that the Lord has taken the initiative, he has loved us first (cf. 1 Jn 4:19), and therefore we can move forward, boldly take the initiative, go out to others, seek those who have fallen away, stand at the crossroads and welcome the outcast. Such a community has an endless desire to show mercy, the fruit of its own experience of the power of the Father's infinite mercy. Let us try a little harder to take the first step and to become involved. Jesus washed the feet of his disciples. The Lord gets involved and he involves his own, as he kneels to wash their feet. He tells his disciples: "You will be blessed if you do this" (Jn 13:17). An evangelizing community gets involved by word and deed in people's daily lives; it bridges distances, it is willing to abase itself if necessary, and it embraces human life, touching the suffering flesh of Christ in others. Evangelizers thus take on the "smell of the sheep" and the sheep are willing to hear their voice. An evangelizing community is also supportive, standing by people at every step of the way, no matter how difficult or lengthy this may prove to be. It is familiar with patient expectation and apostolic endurance. Evangelization consists mostly of patience and disregard for constraints of time. Faithful to the Lord's gift, it also bears fruit. An evangelizing community is always concerned with fruit, because the Lord wants her to be fruitful. It cares for the grain and does not grow impatient at the weeds. The sower, when he sees weeds sprouting among the grain does not grumble or overreact. He or she finds a way to let the word take flesh in a particular situation and bear fruits of new life, however imperfect or incomplete these may appear. The disciple is ready to put his or her whole life on the line, even to accepting martyrdom, in bearing witness to Jesus Christ, yet the goal is not to make enemies but to see God's word accepted and its capacity for liberation and renewal revealed. Finally an evangelizing community is filled with joy; it knows how to rejoice always. It celebrates every small victory, every step forward in the work of evangelization. Evangelization with joy becomes beauty in the liturgy, as part of our daily concern to spread goodness. The Church evangelizes and is herself evangelized through the beauty of the liturgy, which is both a celebration of the task of evangelization and the source of her renewed self-giving.

II. PASTORAL ACTIVITY AND CONVERSION

25. I am aware that nowadays documents do not arouse the same interest as in the past and that they are quickly forgotten. Nevertheless, I want to emphasize that what I am trying to express here has a programmatic significance and important consequences. I hope that all communities will devote the necessary effort to advancing along the path of a pastoral and missionary conversion which cannot leave things as they presently are. "Mere administration"

can no longer be enough.[21] Throughout the world, let us be "permanently in a state of mission".[22]

26. Paul VI invited us to deepen the call to renewal and to make it clear that renewal does not only concern individuals but the entire Church. Let us return to a memorable text which continues to challenge us. "The Church must look with penetrating eyes within herself, ponder the mystery of her own being... This vivid and lively self-awareness inevitably leads to a comparison between the ideal image of the Church as Christ envisaged her and loved her as his holy and spotless bride (cf. Eph 5:27), and the actual image which the Church presents to the world today... This is the source of the Church's heroic and impatient struggle for renewal: the struggle to correct those flaws introduced by her members which her own self-examination, mirroring her exemplar, Christ, points out to her and condemns".[23] The Second Vatican Council presented ecclesial conversion as openness to a constant self-renewal born of fidelity to Jesus Christ: "Every renewal of the Church essentially consists in an increase of fidelity to her own calling... Christ summons the Church as she goes her pilgrim way... to that

---

21. Fifth General Conference of the Latin American and Caribbean Bishops, *Aparecida Document*, 29 June 2007, 201.

22. Ibid., 551.

23. Paul VI, Encyclical Letter Ecclesiam Suam (6 August 1964), 9, 10, 11: AAS 56 (1964), 611-612.

continual reformation of which she always has need, in so far as she is a human institution here on earth".[24]

There are ecclesial structures which can hamper efforts at evangelization, yet even good structures are only helpful when there is a life constantly driving, sustaining and assessing them. Without new life and an authentic evangelical spirit, without the Church's "fidelity to her own calling", any new structure will soon prove ineffective.

An Ecclesial Renewal which Cannot be Deferred

27. I dream of a "missionary option", that is, a missionary impulse capable of transforming everything, so that the Church's customs, ways of doing things, times and schedules, language and structures can be suitably channeled for the evangelization of today's world rather than for her self-preservation. The renewal of structures demanded by pastoral conversion can only be understood in this light: as part of an effort to make them more mission-oriented, to make ordinary pastoral activity on every level more inclusive and open, to inspire in pastoral workers a constant desire to go forth and in this way to elicit a positive response from all those whom Jesus summons to friendship with himself. As John Paul II once said to the Bishops of Oceania: "All renewal in the Church must have mission

---

24. Second Ecumenical Vatican Council, Decree on Ecumenism *Unitatis Redintegratio*, 6.

as its goal if it is not to fall prey to a kind of ecclesial introversion".[25]

28. The parish is not an outdated institution; precisely because it possesses great flexibility, it can assume quite different contours depending on the openness and missionary creativity of the pastor and the community. While certainly not the only institution which evangelizes, if the parish proves capable of self-renewal and constant adaptivity, it continues to be "the Church living in the midst of the homes of her sons and daughters".[26] This presumes that it really is in contact with the homes and the lives of its people, and does not become a useless structure out of touch with people or a self-absorbed group made up of a chosen few. The parish is the presence of the Church in a given territory, an environment for hearing God's word, for growth in the Christian life, for dialogue, proclamation, charitable outreach, worship and celebration.[27] In all its activities the parish encourages and trains its members to be evangelizers.[28] It is a community of communities, a sanctuary where the thirsty come to drink in the midst of their journey, and a centre of constant missionary outreach. We must admit, though, that the call to review and renew our parishes has

25. John Paul II, Post-Synodal Apostolic Exhortation *Ecclesia in Oceania* (22 November 2001), 19: AAS 94 (2002), 390.

26. John Paul II, Post-Synodal Apostolic Exhortation Christifideles Laici (30 September 1988), 26: AAS 81 (1989), 438.

27. Cf. *Propositio* 26.

28. Cf. *Propositio* 44.

not yet sufficed to bring them nearer to people, to make them environments of living communion and participation, and to make them completely mission-oriented.

29. Other Church institutions, basic communities and small communities, movements, and forms of association are a source of enrichment for the Church, raised up by the Spirit for evangelizing different areas and sectors. Frequently they bring a new evangelizing fervour and a new capacity for dialogue with the world whereby the Church is renewed. But it will prove beneficial for them not to lose contact with the rich reality of the local parish and to participate readily in the overall pastoral activity of the particular Church.[29] This kind of integration will prevent them from concentrating only on part of the Gospel or the Church, or becoming nomads without roots.

30. Each particular Church, as a portion of the Catholic Church under the leadership of its bishop, is likewise called to missionary conversion. It is the primary subject of evangelization,[30] since it is the concrete manifestation of the one Church in one specific place, and in it "the one, holy, catholic, and apostolic Church of Christ is truly present and operative".[31] It is the Church incarnate in a certain place, equipped with all the means of salvation bestowed

---

29. Cf. *Propositio* 26.

30. Cf. *Propositio* 41.

31. Second Vatican Ecumenical Council, Decree on the Pastoral Office of Bishops *Christus Dominus*, 11.

by Christ, but with local features. Its joy in communicating Jesus Christ is expressed both by a concern to preach him to areas in greater need and in constantly going forth to the outskirts of its own territory or towards new socio-cultural settings.[32] Wherever the need for the light and the life of the Risen Christ is greatest, it will want to be there.[33] To make this missionary impulse ever more focused, generous and fruitful, I encourage each particular Church to undertake a resolute process of discernment, purification and reform.

31. The bishop must always foster this missionary communion in his diocesan Church, following the ideal of the first Christian communities, in which the believers were of one heart and one soul (cf. Acts 4:32). To do so, he will sometimes go before his people, pointing the way and keeping their hope vibrant. At other times, he will simply be in their midst with his unassuming and merciful presence. At yet other times, he will have to walk after them, helping those who lag behind and – above all – allowing the flock to strike out on new paths. In his mission of fostering a dynamic, open and missionary communion, he will have to encourage and develop the means of participation proposed in the Code of Canon Law,[34] and other forms of pastoral dialogue, out of a desire to listen to everyone and

---

32. Cf. Benedict XVI, Address for the Fortieth Anniversary of the Decree Ad Gentes (11 March 2006): AAS 98 (2006), 337.

33. Cf. *Propositio* 42.

34. Cf. Canons 460-468; 492-502; 511-514; 536-537.

not simply to those who would tell him what he would like to hear. Yet the principal aim of these participatory processes should not be ecclesiastical organization but rather the missionary aspiration of reaching everyone.

32. Since I am called to put into practice what I ask of others, I too must think about a conversion of the papacy. It is my duty, as the Bishop of Rome, to be open to suggestions which can help make the exercise of my ministry more faithful to the meaning which Jesus Christ wished to give it and to the present needs of evangelization. Pope John Paul II asked for help in finding "a way of exercising the primacy which, while in no way renouncing what is essential to its mission, is nonetheless open to a new situation".[35] We have made little progress in this regard. The papacy and the central structures of the universal Church also need to hear the call to pastoral conversion. The Second Vatican Council stated that, like the ancient patriarchal Churches, episcopal conferences are in a position "to contribute in many and fruitful ways to the concrete realization of the collegial spirit".[36] Yet this desire has not been fully realized, since a juridical status of episcopal conferences which would see them as subjects of specific attributions, including genuine doctrinal authority, has not yet been sufficiently elaborat-

---

35. Encyclical Letter Ut Unum Sint (25 May 1995), 95: AAS 87 (1995), 977-978.

36. Second Vatican Ecumenical Council, Dogmatic Constitution on the Church Lumen Gentium, 23.

ed.[37] Excessive centralization, rather than proving helpful, complicates the Church's life and her missionary outreach.

33. Pastoral ministry in a missionary key seeks to abandon the complacent attitude that says: "We have always done it this way". I invite everyone to be bold and creative in this task of rethinking the goals, structures, style and methods of evangelization in their respective communities. A proposal of goals without an adequate communal search for the means of achieving them will inevitably prove illusory. I encourage everyone to apply the guidelines found in this document generously and courageously, without inhibitions or fear. The important thing is to not walk alone, but to rely on each other as brothers and sisters, and especially under the leadership of the bishops, in a wise and realistic pastoral discernment.

III. FROM THE HEART OF THE GOSPEL

34. If we attempt to put all things in a missionary key, this will also affect the way we communicate the message. In today's world of instant communication and occasionally biased media coverage, the message we preach runs a greater risk of being distorted or reduced to some of its secondary aspects. In this way certain issues which are part of the Church's moral teaching are taken out of the con-

---

37. John Paul II, Motu Proprio *Apostolos Suos* (21 May 1998): AAS 90 (1998), 641-658.

text which gives them their meaning. The biggest problem is when the message we preach then seems identified with those secondary aspects which, important as they are, do not in and of themselves convey the heart of Christ's message. We need to be realistic and not assume that our audience understands the full background to what we are saying, or is capable of relating what we say to the very heart of the Gospel which gives it meaning, beauty and attractiveness.

35. Pastoral ministry in a missionary style is not obsessed with the disjointed transmission of a multitude of doctrines to be insistently imposed. When we adopt a pastoral goal and a missionary style which would actually reach everyone without exception or exclusion, the message has to concentrate on the essentials, on what is most beautiful, most grand, most appealing and at the same time most necessary. The message is simplified, while losing none of its depth and truth, and thus becomes all the more forceful and convincing.

36. All revealed truths derive from the same divine source and are to be believed with the same faith, yet some of them are more important for giving direct expression to the heart of the Gospel. In this basic core, what shines forth is the beauty of the saving love of God made manifest in Jesus Christ who died and rose from the dead. In this sense, the Second Vatican Council explained, "in Catholic doctrine there exists an order or a 'hierarchy' of truths,

since they vary in their relation to the foundation of the Christian faith".[38] This holds true as much for the dogmas of faith as for the whole corpus of the Church's teaching, including her moral teaching.

37. Saint Thomas Aquinas taught that the Church's moral teaching has its own "hierarchy", in the virtues and in the acts which proceed from them.[39] What counts above all else is "faith working through love" (Gal 5:6). Works of love directed to one's neighbour are the most perfect external manifestation of the interior grace of the Spirit: "The foundation of the New Law is in the grace of the Holy Spirit, who is manifested in the faith which works through love".[40] Thomas thus explains that, as far as external works are concerned, mercy is the greatest of all the virtues: "In itself mercy is the greatest of the virtues, since all the others revolve around it and, more than this, it makes up for their deficiencies. This is particular to the superior virtue, and as such it is proper to God to have mercy, through which his omnipotence is manifested to the greatest degree".[41]

---

38. Second Vatican Ecumenical Council, Decree on Ecumenism *Unitatis Redintegratio*, 11.

39. Cf. *S. Th.*, I-II, q. 66, a. 4-6.

40. *S. Th.*, I-II, q. 108, a. 1.

41. *S. Th.*, II-II, q. 30, a. 4: "We do not worship God with sacrifices and exterior gifts for him, but rather for us and for our neighbour. He has no need of our sacrifices, but he does ask that these be offered by us as devotion and for the benefit of our neighbour. For him, mercy, which overcomes the defects of our devotion and sacrifice, is the sacrifice which is most pleasing, because it is mercy which above all seeks the good of one's neighbour" (*S. Th.*, II-II, q. 30, a. 4, ad 1).

38. It is important to draw out the pastoral consequences of the Council's teaching, which reflects an ancient conviction of the Church. First, it needs to be said that in preaching the Gospel a fitting sense of proportion has to be maintained. This would be seen in the frequency with which certain themes are brought up and in the emphasis given to them in preaching. For example, if in the course of the liturgical year a parish priest speaks about temperance ten times but only mentions charity or justice two or three times, an imbalance results, and precisely those virtues which ought to be most present in preaching and catechesis are overlooked. The same thing happens when we speak more about law than about grace, more about the Church than about Christ, more about the Pope than about God's word.

39. Just as the organic unity existing among the virtues means that no one of them can be excluded from the Christian ideal, so no truth may be denied. The integrity of the Gospel message must not be deformed. What is more, each truth is better understood when related to the harmonious totality of the Christian message; in this context all of the truths are important and illumine one another. When preaching is faithful to the Gospel, the centrality of certain truths is evident and it becomes clear that Christian morality is not a form of stoicism, or self-denial, or merely a practical philosophy or a catalogue of sins and faults. Before all else, the Gospel invites us to respond to the God of love who saves us, to see God in others and to

go forth from ourselves to seek the good of others. Under no circumstance can this invitation be obscured! All of the virtues are at the service of this response of love. If this invitation does not radiate forcefully and attractively, the edifice of the Church's moral teaching risks becoming a house of cards, and this is our greatest risk. It would mean that it is not the Gospel which is being preached, but certain doctrinal or moral points based on specific ideological options. The message will run the risk of losing its freshness and will cease to have "the fragrance of the Gospel".

IV. A MISSION EMBODIED WITHIN HUMAN LIMITS

40. The Church is herself a missionary disciple; she needs to grow in her interpretation of the revealed word and in her understanding of truth. It is the task of exegetes and theologians to help "the judgment of the Church to mature".[42] The other sciences also help to accomplish this, each in its own way. With reference to the social sciences, for example, John Paul II said that the Church values their research, which helps her "to derive concrete indications helpful for her magisterial mission".[43] Within the Church countless issues are being studied and reflected upon with

---

42. Second Vatican Ecumenical Council, Dogmatic Constitution on Divine Revelation *Dei Verbum*, 12.

43. Motu Proprio *Socialium Scientiarum* (1 January 1994): AAS 86 (1994), 209.

great freedom. Differing currents of thought in philosophy, theology and pastoral practice, if open to being reconciled by the Spirit in respect and love, can enable the Church to grow, since all of them help to express more clearly the immense riches of God's word. For those who long for a monolithic body of doctrine guarded by all and leaving no room for nuance, this might appear as undesirable and leading to confusion. But in fact such variety serves to bring out and develop different facets of the inexhaustible riches of the Gospel.[44]

41. At the same time, today's vast and rapid cultural changes demand that we constantly seek ways of expressing unchanging truths in a language which brings out their abiding newness. "The deposit of the faith is one thing... the way it is expressed is another".[45] There are times when the faithful, in listening to completely orthodox language, take away something alien to the authentic Gospel of Jesus Christ, because that language is alien to their own way of speaking to and understanding one another. With the

---

44. Saint Thomas Aquinas noted that the multiplicity and variety "were the intention of the first agent", who wished that "what each individual thing lacked in order to reflect the divine goodness would be made up for by other things", since the Creator's goodness "could not be fittingly reflected by just one creature" (*S. Th.*, I, q. 47, a. 1). Consequently, we need to grasp the variety of things in their multiple relationships (cf. *S. Th.*, I, q. 47, a. 2, ad 1; q. 47, a. 3). By analogy, we need to listen to and complement one another in our partial reception of reality and the Gospel.

45. John XXIII, Address for the Opening of the Second Vatican Council (11 October 1962): AAS 54 (1962), 792: "*Est enim aliud ipsum depositum fidei, seu veritates, quae veneranda doctrina nostra continentur, aliud modus, quo eaedem enuntiantur*".

holy intent of communicating the truth about God and humanity, we sometimes give them a false god or a human ideal which is not really Christian. In this way, we hold fast to a formulation while failing to convey its substance. This is the greatest danger. Let us never forget that "the expression of truth can take different forms. The renewal of these forms of expression becomes necessary for the sake of transmitting to the people of today the Gospel message in its unchanging meaning".[46]

42. All of this has great relevance for the preaching of the Gospel, if we are really concerned to make its beauty more clearly recognized and accepted by all. Of course, we will never be able to make the Church's teachings easily understood or readily appreciated by everyone. Faith always remains something of a cross; it retains a certain obscurity which does not detract from the firmness of its assent. Some things are understood and appreciated only from the standpoint of this assent, which is a sister to love, beyond the range of clear reasons and arguments. We need to remember that all religious teaching ultimately has to be reflected in the teacher's way of life, which awakens the assent of the heart by its nearness, love and witness.

43. In her ongoing discernment, the Church can also come to see that certain customs not directly connected to the heart of the Gospel, even some which have deep histori-

---

46. John Paul II, Encyclical Letter *Ut Unum Sint* (25 May 1995), 19: AAS 87 (1995), 933.

cal roots, are no longer properly understood and appreciated. Some of these customs may be beautiful, but they no longer serve as means of communicating the Gospel. We should not be afraid to re-examine them. At the same time, the Church has rules or precepts which may have been quite effective in their time, but no longer have the same usefulness for directing and shaping people's lives. Saint Thomas Aquinas pointed out that the precepts which Christ and the apostles gave to the people of God "are very few".[47] Citing Saint Augustine, he noted that the precepts subsequently enjoined by the Church should be insisted upon with moderation "so as not to burden the lives of the faithful" and make our religion a form of servitude, whereas "God's mercy has willed that we should be free".[48] This warning, issued many centuries ago, is most timely today. It ought to be one of the criteria to be taken into account in considering a reform of the Church and her preaching which would enable it to reach everyone.

44. Moreover, pastors and the lay faithful who accompany their brothers and sisters in faith or on a journey of openness to God must always remember what the *Catechism of the Catholic Church* teaches quite clearly: "Imputability and responsibility for an action can be diminished or even nullified by ignorance, inadvertence, duress, fear, habit, inordinate attachments, and other psychological or

---

47. *S. Th.*, I-II, q. 107, a. 4.
48. Ibid.

social factors".[49] Consequently, without detracting from the evangelical ideal, they need to accompany with mercy and patience the eventual stages of personal growth as these progressively occur.[50] I want to remind priests that the confessional must not be a torture chamber but rather an encounter with the Lord's mercy which spurs us on to do our best. A small step, in the midst of great human limitations, can be more pleasing to God than a life which appears outwardly in order but moves through the day without confronting great difficulties. Everyone needs to be touched by the comfort and attraction of God's saving love, which is mysteriously at work in each person, above and beyond their faults and failings.

45. We see then that the task of evangelization operates within the limits of language and of circumstances. It constantly seeks to communicate more effectively the truth of the Gospel in a specific context, without renouncing the truth, the goodness and the light which it can bring whenever perfection is not possible. A missionary heart is aware of these limits and makes itself "weak with the weak... everything for everyone" (1 Cor 9:22). It never closes itself off, never retreats into its own security, never opts for rigidity and defensiveness. It realizes that it has to grow in its own understanding of the Gospel and in discerning the

---

49. No. 1735

50. Cf. John Paul II, Post-Synodal Apostolic Exhortation *Familiaris Consortio* (22 November 1981), 34: AAS 74 (1982), 123.

paths of the Spirit, and so it always does what good it can, even if in the process, its shoes get soiled by the mud of the street.

V. A MOTHER WITH AN OPEN HEART

46. A Church which "goes forth" is a Church whose doors are open. Going out to others in order to reach the fringes of humanity does not mean rushing out aimlessly into the world. Often it is better simply to slow down, to put aside our eagerness in order to see and listen to others, to stop rushing from one thing to another and to remain with someone who has faltered along the way. At times we have to be like the father of the prodigal son, who always keeps his door open so that when the son returns, he can readily pass through it.

47. The Church is called to be the house of the Father, with doors always wide open. One concrete sign of such openness is that our church doors should always be open, so that if someone, moved by the Spirit, comes there looking for God, he or she will not find a closed door. There are other doors that should not be closed either. Everyone can share in some way in the life of the Church; everyone can be part of the community, nor should the doors of the sacraments be closed for simply any reason. This is especially true of the sacrament which is itself "the door": baptism. The Eucharist, although it is the fullness of sacramental

life, is not a prize for the perfect but a powerful medicine and nourishment for the weak.[51] These convictions have pastoral consequences that we are called to consider with prudence and boldness. Frequently, we act as arbiters of grace rather than its facilitators. But the Church is not a tollhouse; it is the house of the Father, where there is a place for everyone, with all their problems.

48. If the whole Church takes up this missionary impulse, she has to go forth to everyone without exception. But to whom should she go first? When we read the Gospel we find a clear indication: not so much our friends and wealthy neighbours, but above all the poor and the sick, those who are usually despised and overlooked, "those who cannot repay you" (Lk 14:14). There can be no room for doubt or for explanations which weaken so clear a message. Today and always, "the poor are the privileged recipients of the Gospel",[52] and the fact that it is freely preached to them is a sign of the kingdom that Jesus came to establish.

---

51. Cf. Saint Ambrose, *De Sacramentis*, IV, 6, 28: PL 16, 464: "I must receive it always, so that it may always forgive my sins. If I sin continually, I must always have a remedy"; ID., op. cit., IV, 5, 24: PL 16, 463: "Those who ate manna died; those who eat this body will obtain the forgiveness of their sins"; Saint Cyril of Alexandria, *In Joh. Evang.*, IV, 2: PG 73, 584-585: "I examined myself and I found myself unworthy. To those who speak thus I say: when will you be worthy? When at last you present yourself before Christ? And if your sins prevent you from drawing nigh, and you never cease to fall – for, as the Psalm says, 'what man knows his faults?' – will you remain without partaking of the sanctification that gives life for eternity?"

52. Benedict XVI, Address to the Brazilian Bishops in the Cathedral of São Paulo, Brazil (11 May 2007), 3: AAS 99 (2007), 428.

We have to state, without mincing words, that there is an inseparable bond between our faith and the poor. May we never abandon them.

49. Let us go forth, then, let us go forth to offer everyone the life of Jesus Christ. Here I repeat for the entire Church what I have often said to the priests and laity of Buenos Aires: I prefer a Church which is bruised, hurting and dirty because it has been out on the streets, rather than a Church which is unhealthy from being confined and from clinging to its own security. I do not want a Church concerned with being at the centre and which then ends by being caught up in a web of obsessions and procedures. If something should rightly disturb us and trouble our consciences, it is the fact that so many of our brothers and sisters are living without the strength, light and consolation born of friendship with Jesus Christ, without a community of faith to support them, without meaning and a goal in life. More than by fear of going astray, my hope is that we will be moved by the fear of remaining shut up within structures which give us a false sense of security, within rules which make us harsh judges, within habits which make us feel safe, while at our door people are starving and Jesus does not tire of saying to us: "Give them something to eat" (Mk 6:37).

CHAPTER TWO

AMID THE CRISIS OF COMMUNAL COMMITMENT

50. Before taking up some basic questions related to the work of evangelization, it may be helpful to mention briefly the context in which we all have to live and work. Today, we frequently hear of a "diagnostic overload" which is not always accompanied by improved and actually applicable methods of treatment. Nor would we be well served by a purely sociological analysis which would aim to embrace all of reality by employing an allegedly neutral and clinical method. What I would like to propose is something much more in the line of an evangelical discernment. It is the approach of a missionary disciple, an approach "nourished by the light and strength of the Holy Spirit".[53]

51. It is not the task of the Pope to offer a detailed and complete analysis of contemporary reality, but I do exhort

---

53. John Paul II, Post-Synodal Apostolic Exhortation *Pastores Dabo Vobis* (25 March 1992), 10: AAS 84 (1992), 673.

all the communities to an "ever watchful scrutiny of the signs of the times".[54] This is in fact a grave responsibility, since certain present realities, unless effectively dealt with, are capable of setting off processes of dehumanization which would then be hard to reverse. We need to distinguish clearly what might be a fruit of the kingdom from what runs counter to God's plan. This involves not only recognizing and discerning spirits, but also – and this is decisive – choosing movements of the spirit of good and rejecting those of the spirit of evil. I take for granted the different analyses which other documents of the universal magisterium have offered, as well as those proposed by the regional and national conferences of bishops. In this Exhortation I claim only to consider briefly, and from a pastoral perspective, certain factors which can restrain or weaken the impulse of missionary renewal in the Church, either because they threaten the life and dignity of God's people or because they affect those who are directly involved in the Church's institutions and in her work of evangelization.

I. SOME CHALLENGES OF TODAY'S WORLD

52. In our time humanity is experiencing a turning-point in its history, as we can see from the advances being made

---

54. Paul VI, Encyclical *Letter Ecclesiam Suam* (6 August 1964), 19: AAS 56 (1964), 609.

in so many fields. We can only praise the steps being taken to improve people's welfare in areas such as health care, education and communications. At the same time we have to remember that the majority of our contemporaries are barely living from day to day, with dire consequences. A number of diseases are spreading. The hearts of many people are gripped by fear and desperation, even in the so-called rich countries. The joy of living frequently fades, lack of respect for others and violence are on the rise, and inequality is increasingly evident. It is a struggle to live and, often, to live with precious little dignity. This epochal change has been set in motion by the enormous qualitative, quantitative, rapid and cumulative advances occurring in the sciences and in technology, and by their instant application in different areas of nature and of life. We are in an age of knowledge and information, which has led to new and often anonymous kinds of power.

No to an Economy of Exclusion

53. Just as the commandment "Thou shalt not kill" sets a clear limit in order to safeguard the value of human life, today we also have to say "thou shalt not" to an economy of exclusion and inequality. Such an economy kills. How can it be that it is not a news item when an elderly homeless person dies of exposure, but it is news when the stock market loses two points? This is a case of exclusion. Can we continue to stand by when food is thrown away while people are starving? This is a case of inequality. Today ev-

erything comes under the laws of competition and the survival of the fittest, where the powerful feed upon the powerless. As a consequence, masses of people find themselves excluded and marginalized: without work, without possibilities, without any means of escape.

Human beings are themselves considered consumer goods to be used and then discarded. We have created a "throw away" culture which is now spreading. It is no longer simply about exploitation and oppression, but something new. Exclusion ultimately has to do with what it means to be a part of the society in which we live; those excluded are no longer society's underside or its fringes or its disenfranchised – they are no longer even a part of it. The excluded are not the "exploited" but the outcast, the "leftovers".

54. In this context, some people continue to defend trickle-down theories which assume that economic growth, encouraged by a free market, will inevitably succeed in bringing about greater justice and inclusiveness in the world. This opinion, which has never been confirmed by the facts, expresses a crude and naïve trust in the goodness of those wielding economic power and in the sacralized workings of the prevailing economic system. Meanwhile, the excluded are still waiting. To sustain a lifestyle which excludes others, or to sustain enthusiasm for that selfish ideal, a globalization of indifference has developed. Almost without being aware of it, we end up being incapable of feeling compassion at the outcry of the poor, weeping for other people's pain, and feeling a need to help them, as though

all this were someone else's responsibility and not our own. The culture of prosperity deadens us; we are thrilled if the market offers us something new to purchase. In the meantime all those lives stunted for lack of opportunity seem a mere spectacle; they fail to move us.

No to the New Idolatry of Money

55. One cause of this situation is found in our relationship with money, since we calmly accept its dominion over ourselves and our societies. The current financial crisis can make us overlook the fact that it originated in a profound human crisis: the denial of the primacy of the human person! We have created new idols. The worship of the ancient golden calf (cf. Ex 32:1-35) has returned in a new and ruthless guise in the idolatry of money and the dictatorship of an impersonal economy lacking a truly human purpose. The worldwide crisis affecting finance and the economy lays bare their imbalances and, above all, their lack of real concern for human beings; man is reduced to one of his needs alone: consumption.

56. While the earnings of a minority are growing exponentially, so too is the gap separating the majority from the prosperity enjoyed by those happy few. This imbalance is the result of ideologies which defend the absolute autonomy of the marketplace and financial speculation. Consequently, they reject the right of states, charged with vigilance for the common good, to exercise any form of

control. A new tyranny is thus born, invisible and often virtual, which unilaterally and relentlessly imposes its own laws and rules. Debt and the accumulation of interest also make it difficult for countries to realize the potential of their own economies and keep citizens from enjoying their real purchasing power. To all this we can add widespread corruption and self-serving tax evasion, which have taken on worldwide dimensions. The thirst for power and possessions knows no limits. In this system, which tends to devour everything which stands in the way of increased profits, whatever is fragile, like the environment, is defenseless before the interests of a deified market, which become the only rule.

No to a Financial System which Rules Rather than Serves

57. Behind this attitude lurks a rejection of ethics and a rejection of God. Ethics has come to be viewed with a certain scornful derision. It is seen as counterproductive, too human, because it makes money and power relative. It is felt to be a threat, since it condemns the manipulation and debasement of the person. In effect, ethics leads to a God who calls for a committed response which is outside the categories of the marketplace. When these latter are absolutized, God can only be seen as uncontrollable, unmanageable, even dangerous, since he calls human beings to their full realization and to freedom from all forms of enslavement. Ethics – a non-ideological ethics – would

make it possible to bring about balance and a more humane social order. With this in mind, I encourage financial experts and political leaders to ponder the words of one of the sages of antiquity: "Not to share one's wealth with the poor is to steal from them and to take away their livelihood. It is not our own goods which we hold, but theirs".[55]

58. A financial reform open to such ethical considerations would require a vigorous change of approach on the part of political leaders. I urge them to face this challenge with determination and an eye to the future, while not ignoring, of course, the specifics of each case. Money must serve, not rule! The Pope loves everyone, rich and poor alike, but he is obliged in the name of Christ to remind all that the rich must help, respect and promote the poor. I exhort you to generous solidarity and to the return of economics and finance to an ethical approach which favours human beings.

No to the Inequality which Spawns Violence

59. Today in many places we hear a call for greater security. But until exclusion and inequality in society and between peoples are reversed, it will be impossible to eliminate violence. The poor and the poorer peoples are accused of violence, yet without equal opportunities the different forms of aggression and conflict will find a fertile terrain for growth and eventually explode. When a society – whether

---

55. Saint John Chrysostom, *De Lazaro Concio*, II, 6: PG 48, 992D.

local, national or global – is willing to leave a part of itself on the fringes, no political programmes or resources spent on law enforcement or surveillance systems can indefinitely guarantee tranquility. This is not the case simply because inequality provokes a violent reaction from those excluded from the system, but because the socioeconomic system is unjust at its root. Just as goodness tends to spread, the toleration of evil, which is injustice, tends to expand its baneful influence and quietly to undermine any political and social system, no matter how solid it may appear. If every action has its consequences, an evil embedded in the structures of a society has a constant potential for disintegration and death. It is evil crystallized in unjust social structures, which cannot be the basis of hope for a better future. We are far from the so-called "end of history", since the conditions for a sustainable and peaceful development have not yet been adequately articulated and realized.

60. Today's economic mechanisms promote inordinate consumption, yet it is evident that unbridled consumerism combined with inequality proves doubly damaging to the social fabric. Inequality eventually engenders a violence which recourse to arms cannot and never will be able to resolve. It serves only to offer false hopes to those clamouring for heightened security, even though nowadays we know that weapons and violence, rather than providing solutions, create new and more serious conflicts. Some simply content themselves with blaming the poor and the poorer countries themselves for their troubles; indulging in unwarranted generalizations, they claim that the solution is

an "education" that would tranquilize them, making them tame and harmless. All this becomes even more exasperating for the marginalized in the light of the widespread and deeply rooted corruption found in many countries – in their governments, businesses and institutions – whatever the political ideology of their leaders.

Some Cultural Challenges

61. We also evangelize when we attempt to confront the various challenges which can arise.[56] On occasion these may take the form of veritable attacks on religious freedom or new persecutions directed against Christians; in some countries these have reached alarming levels of hatred and violence. In many places, the problem is more that of widespread indifference and relativism, linked to disillusionment and the crisis of ideologies which has come about as a reaction to any-thing which might appear totalitarian. This not only harms the Church but the fabric of society as a whole. We should recognize how in a culture where each person wants to be bearer of his or her own subjective truth, it becomes difficult for citizens to devise a common plan which transcends individual gain and personal ambitions.

62. In the prevailing culture, priority is given to the outward, the immediate, the visible, the quick, the superficial

---

56. Cf. *Propositio* 13.

and the provisional. What is real gives way to appearances. In many countries globalization has meant a hastened deterioration of their own cultural roots and the invasion of ways of thinking and acting proper to other cultures which are economically advanced but ethically debilitated. This fact has been brought up by bishops from various continents in different Synods. The African bishops, for example, taking up the Encyclical *Sollicitudo Rei Socialis*, pointed out years ago that there have been frequent attempts to make the African countries "parts of a machine, cogs on a gigantic wheel. This is often true also in the field of social communications which, being run by centres mostly in the northern hemisphere, do not always give due consideration to the priorities and problems of such countries or respect their cultural make-up".[57] By the same token, the bishops of Asia "underlined the external influences being brought to bear on Asian cultures. New patterns of behaviour are emerging as a result of over-exposure to the mass media… As a result, the negative aspects of the media and entertainment industries are threatening traditional values, and in particular the sacredness of marriage and the stability of the family".[58]

---

57. John Paul II, Apostolic Exhortation *Ecclesia in Africa* (14 September 1995), 52: AAS 88 (1996), 32-33; ID. , Encyclical Letter *Sollicitudo Rei Socialis* (30 December 1987), 22: AAS 80 (1988), 539.

58. John Paul II, Apostolic Exhortation *Ecclesia in Asia* (6 November 1999), 7: AAS 92 (2000), 458.

63. The Catholic faith of many peoples is nowadays being challenged by the proliferation of new religious movements, some of which tend to fundamentalism while others seem to propose a spirituality without God. This is, on the one hand, a human reaction to a materialistic, consumerist and individualistic society, but it is also a means of exploiting the weaknesses of people living in poverty and on the fringes of society, people who make ends meet amid great human suffering and are looking for immediate solutions to their needs. These religious movements, not without a certain shrewdness, come to fill, within a predominantly individualistic culture, a vacuum left by secularist rationalism. We must recognize that if part of our baptized people lack a sense of belonging to the Church, this is also due to certain structures and the occasionally unwelcoming atmosphere of some of our parishes and communities, or to a bureaucratic way of dealing with problems, be they simple or complex, in the lives of our people. In many places an administrative approach prevails over a pastoral approach, as does a concentration on administering the sacraments apart from other forms of evangelization.

64. The process of secularization tends to reduce the faith and the Church to the sphere of the private and personal. Furthermore, by completely rejecting the transcendent, it has produced a growing deterioration of ethics, a weakening of the sense of personal and collective sin, and a steady increase in relativism. These have led to a general sense of disorientation, especially in the periods of adolescence and

young adulthood which are so vulnerable to change. As the bishops of the United States of America have rightly pointed out, while the Church insists on the existence of objective moral norms which are valid for everyone, "there are those in our culture who portray this teaching as unjust, that is, as opposed to basic human rights. Such claims usually follow from a form of moral relativism that is joined, not without inconsistency, to a belief in the absolute rights of individuals. In this view, the Church is perceived as promoting a particular prejudice and as interfering with individual freedom".[59] We are living in an information-driven society which bombards us indiscriminately with data – all treated as being of equal importance – and which leads to remarkable superficiality in the area of moral discernment. In response, we need to provide an education which teaches critical thinking and encourages the development of mature moral values.

65. Despite the tide of secularism which has swept our societies, in many countries – even those where Christians are a minority – the Catholic Church is considered a credible institution by public opinion, and trusted for her solidarity and concern for those in greatest need. Again and again, the Church has acted as a mediator in finding solutions to problems affecting peace, social harmony, the land, the defence of life, human and civil rights, and so

---

59. United States Conference Of Catholic Bishops, Ministry to *Persons with a Homosexual Inclination: Guidelines for Pastoral Care* (2006), 17.

forth. And how much good has been done by Catholic schools and universities around the world! This is a good thing. Yet, we find it difficult to make people see that when we raise other questions less palatable to public opinion, we are doing so out of fidelity to precisely the same convictions about human dignity and the common good.

66. The family is experiencing a profound cultural crisis, as are all communities and social bonds. In the case of the family, the weakening of these bonds is particularly serious because the family is the fundamental cell of society, where we learn to live with others despite our differences and to belong to one another; it is also the place where parents pass on the faith to their children. Marriage now tends to be viewed as a form of mere emotional satisfaction that can be constructed in any way or modified at will. But the indispensable contribution of marriage to society transcends the feelings and momentary needs of the couple. As the French bishops have taught, it is not born "of loving sentiment, ephemeral by definition, but from the depth of the obligation assumed by the spouses who accept to enter a total communion of life".[60]

67. The individualism of our postmodern and globalized era favours a lifestyle which weakens the development and stability of personal relationships and distorts family

---

60. Conférence Des Évêques De France, Conseil Famille et Société, *Élargir le mariage aux personnes de même sexe? Ouvrons le débat!* (28 September 2012).

bonds. Pastoral activity needs to bring out more clearly the fact that our relationship with the Father demands and encourages a communion which heals, promotes and reinforces interpersonal bonds. In our world, especially in some countries, different forms of war and conflict are re-emerging, yet we Christians remain steadfast in our intention to respect others, to heal wounds, to build bridges, to strengthen relationships and to "bear one another's burdens" (Gal 6:2). Today too, various associations for the defence of rights and the pursuit of noble goals are being founded. This is a sign of the desire of many people to contribute to social and cultural progress.

Challenges to Inculturating the Faith

68. The Christian substratum of certain peoples – most of all in the West – is a living reality. Here we find, especially among the most needy, a moral resource which preserves the values of an authentic Christian humanism. Seeing reality with the eyes of faith, we cannot fail to acknowledge what the Holy Spirit is sowing. It would show a lack of trust in his free and unstinting activity to think that authentic Christian values are absent where great numbers of people have received baptism and express their faith and solidarity with others in a variety of ways. This means more than acknowledging occasional "seeds of the word", since it has to do with an authentic Christian faith which has its own expressions and means of showing its relationship to the Church. The immense importance of a culture marked

by faith cannot be overlooked; before the onslaught of contemporary secularism an evangelized culture, for all its limits, has many more resources than the mere sum total of believers. An evangelized popular culture contains values of faith and solidarity capable of encouraging the development of a more just and believing society, and possesses a particular wisdom which ought to be gratefully acknowledged.

69. It is imperative to evangelize cultures in order to inculturate the Gospel. In countries of Catholic tradition, this means encouraging, fostering and reinforcing a richness which already exists. In countries of other religious traditions, or profoundly secularized countries, it will mean sparking new processes for evangelizing culture, even though these will demand long-term planning. We must keep in mind, however, that we are constantly being called to grow. Each culture and social group needs purification and growth. In the case of the popular cultures of Catholic peoples, we can see deficiencies which need to be healed by the Gospel: machismo, alcoholism, domestic violence, low Mass attendance, fatalistic or superstitious notions which lead to sorcery, and the like. Popular piety itself can be the starting point for healing and liberation from these deficiencies.

70. It is also true that at times greater emphasis is placed on the outward expressions and traditions of some groups, or on alleged private revelations which would replace all

else, than on the impulse of Christian piety. There is a kind of Christianity made up of devotions reflecting an individual and sentimental faith life which does not in fact correspond to authentic "popular piety". Some people promote these expressions while not being in the least concerned with the advancement of society or the formation of the laity, and in certain cases they do so in order to obtain economic benefits or some power over others. Nor can we overlook the fact that in recent decades there has been a breakdown in the way Catholics pass down the Christian faith to the young. It is undeniable that many people feel disillusioned and no longer identify with the Catholic tradition. Growing numbers of parents do not bring their children for baptism or teach them how to pray. There is also a certain exodus towards other faith communities. The causes of this breakdown include: a lack of opportunity for dialogue in families, the influence of the communications media, a relativistic subjectivism, unbridled consumerism which feeds the market, lack of pastoral care among the poor, the failure of our institutions to be welcoming, and our difficulty in restoring a mystical adherence to the faith in a pluralistic religious landscape.

Challenges from Urban Cultures

71. The new Jerusalem, the holy city (cf. Rev 21:2-4), is the goal towards which all of humanity is moving. It is curious that God's revelation tells us that the fullness of humanity and of history is realized in a city. We need to

look at our cities with a contemplative gaze, a gaze of faith which sees God dwelling in their homes, in their streets and squares. God's presence accompanies the sincere efforts of individuals and groups to find encouragement and meaning in their lives. He dwells among them, fostering solidarity, fraternity, and the desire for goodness, truth and justice. This presence must not be contrived but found, uncovered. God does not hide himself from those who seek him with a sincere heart, even though they do so tentatively, in a vague and haphazard manner.

72. In cities, as opposed to the countryside, the religious dimension of life is expressed by different lifestyles, daily rhythms linked to places and people. In their daily lives people must often struggle for survival and this struggle contains within it a profound understanding of life which often includes a deep religious sense. We must examine this more closely in order to enter into a dialogue like that of our Lord and the Samaritan woman at the well where she sought to quench her thirst (cf. Jn 4:1-15).

73. New cultures are constantly being born in these vast new expanses where Christians are no longer the customary interpreters or generators of meaning. Instead, they themselves take from these cultures new languages, symbols, messages and paradigms which propose new approaches to life, approaches often in contrast with the Gospel of Jesus. A completely new culture has come to life and continues to grow in the cities. The Synod noted that

today the changes taking place in these great spaces and the culture which they create are a privileged locus of the new evangelization.[61] This challenges us to imagine innovative spaces and possibilities for prayer and communion which are more attractive and meaningful for city dwellers. Through the influence of the media, rural areas are being affected by the same cultural changes, which are significantly altering their way of life as well.

74. What is called for is an evangelization capable of shedding light on these new ways of relating to God, to others and to the world around us, and inspiring essential values. It must reach the places where new narratives and paradigms are being formed, bringing the word of Jesus to the inmost soul of our cities. Cities are multicultural; in the larger cities, a connective network is found in which groups of people share a common imagination and dreams about life, and new human interactions arise, new cultures, invisible cities. Various subcultures exist side by side, and often practise segregation and violence. The Church is called to be at the service of a difficult dialogue. On the one hand, there are people who have the means needed to develop their personal and family lives, but there are also many "non-citizens", "half citizens" and "urban remnants". Cities create a sort of permanent ambivalence because, while they offer their residents countless possibilities, they also present many people with any number of obstacles to the

61. Cf. *Propositio* 25.

full development of their lives. This contrast causes painful suffering. In many parts of the world, cities are the scene of mass protests where thousands of people call for freedom, a voice in public life, justice and a variety of other demands which, if not properly understood, will not be silenced by force.

75. We cannot ignore the fact that in cities human trafficking, the narcotics trade, the abuse and exploitation of minors, the abandonment of the elderly and infirm, and various forms of corruption and criminal activity take place. At the same time, what could be significant places of encounter and solidarity often become places of isolation and mutual distrust. Houses and neighbourhoods are more often built to isolate and protect than to connect and integrate. The proclamation of the Gospel will be a basis for restoring the dignity of human life in these contexts, for Jesus desires to pour out an abundance of life upon our cities (cf. Jn 10:10). The unified and complete sense of human life that the Gospel proposes is the best remedy for the ills of our cities, even though we have to realize that a uniform and rigid program of evangelization is not suited to this complex reality. But to live our human life to the fullest and to meet every challenge as a leaven of Gospel witness in every culture and in every city will make us better Christians and bear fruit in our cities.

II. TEMPTATIONS FACED BY PASTORAL WORKERS

76. I feel tremendous gratitude to all those who are committed to working in and for the Church. Here I do not wish to discuss at length the activities of the different pastoral workers, from bishops down to those who provide the most humble and hidden services. Rather, I would like to reflect on the challenges that all of them must face in the context of our current globalized culture. But in justice, I must say first that the contribution of the Church in today's world is enormous. The pain and the shame we feel at the sins of some members of the Church, and at our own, must never make us forget how many Christians are giving their lives in love. They help so many people to be healed or to die in peace in makeshift hospitals. They are present to those enslaved by different addictions in the poorest places on earth. They devote themselves to the education of children and young people. They take care of the elderly who have been forgotten by everyone else. They look for ways to communicate values in hostile environments. They are dedicated in many other ways to showing an immense love for humanity inspired by the God who became man. I am grateful for the beautiful example given to me by so many Christians who joyfully sacrifice their lives and their time. This witness comforts and sustains me in my own effort to overcome selfishness and to give more fully of myself.

77. As children of this age, though, all of us are in some way affected by the present globalized culture which, while offering us values and new possibilities, can also limit, condition and ultimately harm us. I am aware that we need to create spaces where pastoral workers can be helped and healed, "places where faith itself in the crucified and risen Jesus is renewed, where the most profound questions and daily concerns are shared, where deeper discernment about our experiences and life itself is undertaken in the light of the Gospel, for the purpose of directing individual and social decisions towards the good and beautiful".[62] At the same time, I would like to call attention to certain particular temptations which affect pastoral workers.

Yes to the Challenge of a Missionary Spirituality

78. Today we are seeing in many pastoral workers, including consecrated men and women, an inordinate concern for their personal freedom and relaxation, which leads them to see their work as a mere appendage to their life, as if it were not part of their very identity. At the same time, the spiritual life comes to be identified with a few religious exercises which can offer a certain comfort but which do not encourage encounter with others, engagement with the world or a passion for evangelization. As a result, one

---

62. Azione Cattolica Italiana, *Messaggio della XIV Assemblea Nazionale alla Chiesa ed al Paese* (8 May 2011).

can observe in many agents of evangelization, even though they pray, a heightened individualism, a crisis of identity and a cooling of fervour. These are three evils which fuel one another.

79. At times our media culture and some intellectual circles convey a marked scepticism with regard to the Church's message, along with a certain cynicism. As a consequence, many pastoral workers, although they pray, develop a sort of inferiority complex which leads them to relativize or conceal their Christian identity and convictions. This produces a vicious circle. They end up being unhappy with who they are and what they do; they do not identify with their mission of evangelization and this weakens their commitment. They end up stifling the joy of mission with a kind of obsession about being like everyone else and possessing what everyone else possesses. Their work of evangelization thus becomes forced, and they devote little energy and very limited time to it.

80. Pastoral workers can thus fall into a relativism which, whatever their particular style of spirituality or way of thinking, proves even more dangerous than doctrinal relativism. It has to do with the deepest and inmost decisions that shape their way of life. This practical relativism consists in acting as if God did not exist, making decisions as if the poor did not exist, setting goals as if others did not exist, working as if people who have not received the Gospel did not exist. It is striking that even some who clearly have

solid doctrinal and spiritual convictions frequently fall into a lifestyle which leads to an attachment to financial security, or to a desire for power or human glory at all cost, rather than giving their lives to others in mission. Let us not allow ourselves to be robbed of missionary enthusiasm!

No to Selfishness and Spiritual Sloth

81. At a time when we most need a missionary dynamism which will bring salt and light to the world, many lay people fear that they may be asked to undertake some apostolic work and they seek to avoid any responsibility that may take away from their free time. For example, it has become very difficult today to find trained parish catechists willing to persevere in this work for some years. Something similar is also happening with priests who are obsessed with protecting their free time. This is frequently due to the fact that people feel an overbearing need to guard their personal freedom, as though the task of evangelization was a dangerous poison rather than a joyful response to God's love which summons us to mission and makes us fulfilled and productive. Some resist giving themselves over completely to mission and thus end up in a state of paralysis and acedia.

82. The problem is not always an excess of activity, but rather activity undertaken badly, without adequate motivation, without a spirituality which would permeate it and make it pleasurable. As a result, work becomes more tiring than necessary, even leading at times to illness. Far from a

content and happy tiredness, this is a tense, burdensome, dissatisfying and, in the end, unbearable fatigue. This pastoral acedia can be caused by a number of things. Some fall into it because they throw themselves into unrealistic projects and are not satisfied simply to do what they reasonably can. Others, because they lack the patience to allow processes to mature; they want everything to fall from heaven. Others, because they are attached to a few projects or vain dreams of success. Others, because they have lost real contract with people and so depersonalize their work that they are more concerned with the road map than with the journey itself. Others fall into acedia because they are unable to wait; they want to dominate the rhythm of life. Today's obsession with immediate results makes it hard for pastoral workers to tolerate anything that smacks of disagreement, possible failure, criticism, the cross.

83. And so the biggest threat of all gradually takes shape: "the gray pragmatism of the daily life of the Church, in which all appears to proceed normally, while in reality faith is wearing down and degenerating into small-mindedness".[63] A tomb psychology thus develops and slowly transforms Christians into mummies in a museum. Disillusioned with reality, with the Church and with them-

---

63. J. Ratzinger, *The Current Situation of Faith and Theology*. Conference given at the Meeting of Presidents of Latin American Episcopal Commissions for the Doctrine of the Faith, Guadalajara, Mexico, 1996. Translation in L'Osservatore Romano, English Language Edition, 6 November 1996. Cf. Fifth General Conference of the Latin American and Caribbean Bishops, Aparecida Document, 29 June 2007, 12.

selves, they experience a constant temptation to cling to a faint melancholy, lacking in hope, which seizes the heart like "the most precious of the devil's potions".[64] Called to radiate light and communicate life, in the end they are caught up in things that generate only darkness and inner weariness, and slowly consume all zeal for the apostolate. For all this, I repeat: Let us not allow ourselves to be robbed of the joy of evangelization!

No to a Sterile Pessimism

84. The joy of the Gospel is such that it cannot be taken away from us by anyone or anything (cf. Jn 16:22). The evils of our world – and those of the Church – must not be excuses for diminishing our commitment and our fervour. Let us look upon them as challenges which can help us to grow. With the eyes of faith, we can see the light which the Holy Spirit always radiates in the midst of darkness, never forgetting that "where sin increased, grace has abounded all the more" (Rom 5:20). Our faith is challenged to discern how wine can come from water and how wheat can grow in the midst of weeds. Fifty years after the Second Vatican Council, we are distressed by the troubles of our age and far from naive optimism; yet the fact that we are more realistic must not mean that we are any less trusting in the Spirit or less generous. In this sense, we can once again listen to the words of Blessed John XXIII on the memorable

---

64. G. Bernanos, *Journal d'un curé de campagne*, Paris, 1974, 135.

day of 11 October 1962: "At times we have to listen, much to our regret, to the voices of people who, though burning with zeal, lack a sense of discretion and measure. In this modern age they can see nothing but prevarication and ruin … We feel that we must disagree with those prophets of doom who are always forecasting disaster, as though the end of the world were at hand. In our times, divine Providence is leading us to a new order of human relations which, by human effort and even beyond all expectations, are directed to the fulfilment of God's superior and inscrutable designs, in which everything, even human setbacks, leads to the greater good of the Church".[65]

85. One of the more serious temptations which stifles boldness and zeal is a defeatism which turns us into querulous and disillusioned pessimists, "sourpusses". Nobody can go off to battle unless he is fully convinced of victory beforehand. If we start without confidence, we have already lost half the battle and we bury our talents. While painfully aware of our own frailties, we have to march on without giving in, keeping in mind what the Lord said to Saint Paul: "My grace is sufficient for you, for my power is made perfect in weakness" (2 Cor 12:9). Christian triumph is always a cross, yet a cross which is at the same time a victorious banner borne with aggressive tenderness against the assaults of evil. The evil spirit of defeatism is brother to the temptation to separate, before its time, the

---

65. Address for the Opening of the Second Vatican Council (11 October 1962): 4, 2-4: AAS 54 (1962), 789.

wheat from the weeds; it is the fruit of an anxious and self-centred lack of trust.

86. In some places a spiritual "desertification" has evidently come about, as the result of attempts by some societies to build without God or to eliminate their Christian roots. In those places "the Christian world is becoming sterile, and it is depleting itself like an overexploited ground, which transforms into a desert".[66] In other countries, violent opposition to Christianity forces Christians to hide their faith in their own beloved homeland. This is another painful kind of desert. But family and the workplace can also be a parched place where faith nonetheless has to be preserved and communicated. Yet "it is starting from the experience of this desert, from this void, that we can again discover the joy of believing, its vital importance for us men and women. In the desert we rediscover the value of what is essential for living; thus in today's world there are innumerable signs, often expressed implicitly or negatively, of the thirst for God, for the ultimate meaning of life. And in the desert people of faith are needed who, by the example of their own lives, point out the way to the Promised Land and keep hope alive".[67] In these situations we are called to be living sources of water from which others can drink. At times, this becomes a heavy cross, but it was from the

---

66. J.H. Newman, Letter of 26 January 1833, in *The Letters and Diaries of John Henry Newman*, vol. III, Oxford, 1979, 204.

67. Benedict XVI, Homily at Mass for the Opening of the Year of Faith (11 October 2012): AAS 104 (2012), 881.

cross, from his pierced side, that our Lord gave himself to us as a source of living water. Let us not allow ourselves to be robbed of hope!

Yes to the New Relationships Brought by Christ

87. Today, when the networks and means of human communication have made unprecedented advances, we sense the challenge of finding and sharing a "mystique" of living together, of mingling and encounter, of embracing and supporting one another, of stepping into this flood tide which, while chaotic, can become a genuine experience of fraternity, a caravan of solidarity, a sacred pilgrimage. Greater possibilities for communication thus turn into greater possibilities for encounter and solidarity for everyone. If we were able to take this route, it would be so good, so soothing, so liberating and hope-filled! To go out of ourselves and to join others is healthy for us. To be self-enclosed is to taste the bitter poison of immanence, and humanity will be worse for every selfish choice we make.

88. The Christian ideal will always be a summons to overcome suspicion, habitual mistrust, fear of losing our privacy, all the defensive attitudes which today's world imposes on us. Many try to escape from others and take refuge in the comfort of their privacy or in a small circle of close friends, renouncing the realism of the social aspect of the Gospel. For just as some people want a purely spiritual Christ, without flesh and without the cross, they also want their interpersonal relationships provided by sophisticated

equipment, by screens and systems which can be turned on and off on command. Meanwhile, the Gospel tells us constantly to run the risk of a face-to-face encounter with others, with their physical presence which challenges us, with their pain and their pleas, with their joy which infects us in our close and continuous interaction. True faith in the incarnate Son of God is inseparable from self-giving, from membership in the community, from service, from reconciliation with others. The Son of God, by becoming flesh, summoned us to the revolution of tenderness.

89. Isolation, which is a version of immanentism, can find expression in a false autonomy which has no place for God. But in the realm of religion it can also take the form of a spiritual consumerism tailored to one's own unhealthy individualism. The return to the sacred and the quest for spirituality which mark our own time are ambiguous phenomena. Today, our challenge is not so much atheism as the need to respond adequately to many people's thirst for God, lest they try to satisfy it with alienating solutions or with a disembodied Jesus who demands nothing of us with regard to others. Unless these people find in the Church a spirituality which can offer healing and liberation, and fill them with life and peace, while at the same time summoning them to fraternal communion and missionary fruitfulness, they will end up by being taken in by solutions which neither make life truly human nor give glory to God.

90. Genuine forms of popular religiosity are incarnate, since they are born of the incarnation of Christian faith in

popular culture. For this reason they entail a personal relationship, not with vague spiritual energies or powers, but with God, with Christ, with Mary, with the saints. These devotions are fleshy, they have a face. They are capable of fostering relationships and not just enabling escapism. In other parts of our society, we see the growing attraction to various forms of a "spirituality of well-being" divorced from any community life, or to a "theology of prosperity" detached from responsibility for our brothers and sisters, or to depersonalized experiences which are nothing more than a form of self-centredness.

91. One important challenge is to show that the solution will never be found in fleeing from a personal and committed relationship with God which at the same time commits us to serving others. This happens frequently nowadays, as believers seek to hide or keep apart from others, or quietly flit from one place to another or from one task to another, without creating deep and stable bonds. *"Imaginatio locorum et mutatio multos fefellit"*.[68] This is a false remedy which cripples the heart and at times the body as well. We need to help others to realize that the only way is to learn how to encounter others with the right attitude, which is to accept and esteem them as companions along the way, without interior resistance. Better yet, it means learning to find Jesus in the faces of others, in their voices, in their pleas. And learning to suffer in the embrace of the crucified Jesus

---

68. Thomas À Kempis, De Imitatione Christi, Lib. I, IX, 5: "Dreaming of different places, and moving from one to another, has misled many".

whenever we are unjustly attacked or meet with ingratitude, never tiring of our decision to live in fraternity.[69]

92. There indeed we find true healing, since the way to relate to others which truly heals instead of debilitating us, is a mystical fraternity, a contemplative fraternity. It is a fraternal love capable of seeing the sacred grandeur of our neighbour, of finding God in every human being, of tolerating the nuisances of life in common by clinging to the love of God, of opening the heart to divine love and seeking the happiness of others just as their heavenly Father does. Here and now, especially where we are a "little flock" (Lk 12:32), the Lord's disciples are called to live as a community which is the salt of the earth and the light of the world (cf. Mt 5:13-16). We are called to bear witness to a constantly new way of living together in fidelity to the Gospel.[70] Let us not allow ourselves to be robbed of community!

---

69. We can benefit from the testimony of Saint Thérèse of Lisieux, who speaks of one particular Sister whom she found especially disagreeable, where an interior experience had a decisive impact: "One winter afternoon I was engaged as usual in my little task. It was cold and growing dark... Suddenly I heard in the distance the harmonious sounds of a musical instrument. I began to imagine a well-lit room, draped in gold, and in it, elegantly dressed young ladies exchanging worldly compliments and courtesies. Then I looked at the poor sick woman whom I was attending. In place of a melody, I heard her occasional groans and sighs... I cannot express what took place in my soul. All that I do know is that the Lord illuminated it with the rays of truth which so surpassed the flickering glow of earthly revels, that I could scarcely believe my happiness" (Ms. C, 29v-30r, in Oeuvres Complètes, Paris, 1992, 274-275).

70. Cf. *Propositio* 8.

No to Spiritual Worldliness

93. Spiritual worldliness, which hides behind the appearance of piety and even love for the Church, consists in seeking not the Lord's glory but human glory and personal well-being. It is what the Lord reprimanded the Pharisees for: "How can you believe, who receive glory from one another and do not seek the glory that comes from the only God?" (Jn 5:44). It is a subtle way of seeking one's "own interests, not those of Jesus Christ" (Phil 2:21). It takes on many forms, depending on the kinds of persons and groups into which it seeps. Since it is based on carefully cultivated appearances, it is not always linked to outward sin; from without, everything appears as it should be. But if it were to seep into the Church, "it would be infinitely more disastrous than any other worldliness which is simply moral".[71]

94. This worldliness can be fuelled in two deeply interrelated ways. One is the attraction of gnosticism, a purely subjective faith whose only interest is a certain experience or a set of ideas and bits of information which are meant to console and enlighten, but which ultimately keep one imprisoned in his or her own thoughts and feelings. The other is the self-absorbed promethean neopelagianism of those who ultimately trust only in their own powers and feel superior to others because they observe certain rules or remain intransigently faithful to a particular Catholic

---

71. H. De Lubac, *Méditation sur l'Église*, Paris, 1968, 321.

style from the past. A supposed soundness of doctrine or discipline leads instead to a narcissistic and authoritarian elitism, whereby instead of evangelizing, one analyzes and classifies others, and instead of opening the door to grace, one exhausts his or her energies in inspecting and verifying. In neither case is one really concerned about Jesus Christ or others. These are manifestations of an anthropocentric immanentism. It is impossible to think that a genuine evangelizing thrust could emerge from these adulterated forms of Christianity.

95. This insidious worldliness is evident in a number of attitudes which appear opposed, yet all have the same pretence of "taking over the space of the Church". In some people we see an ostentatious preoccupation for the liturgy, for doctrine and for the Church's prestige, but without any concern that the Gospel have a real impact on God's faithful people and the concrete needs of the present time. In this way, the life of the Church turns into a museum piece or something which is the property of a select few. In others, this spiritual worldliness lurks behind a fascination with social and political gain, or pride in their ability to manage practical affairs, or an obsession with programmes of self-help and self-realization. It can also translate into a concern to be seen, into a social life full of appearances, meetings, dinners and receptions. It can also lead to a business mentality, caught up with management, statistics, plans and evaluations whose principal beneficiary is not God's people but the Church as an institution. The mark of Christ, incarnate, crucified and risen, is not pres-

ent; closed and elite groups are formed, and no effort is made to go forth and seek out those who are distant or the immense multitudes who thirst for Christ. Evangelical fervour is replaced by the empty pleasure of complacency and self-indulgence.

96. This way of thinking also feeds the vainglory of those who are content to have a modicum of power and would rather be the general of a defeated army than a mere private in a unit which continues to fight. How often we dream up vast apostolic projects, meticulously planned, just like defeated generals! But this is to deny our history as a Church, which is glorious precisely because it is a history of sacrifice, of hopes and daily struggles, of lives spent in service and fidelity to work, tiring as it may be, for all work is "the sweat of our brow". Instead, we waste time talking about "what needs to be done" – in Spanish we call this the sin of "habriaqueísmo" – like spiritual masters and pastoral experts who give instructions from on high. We indulge in endless fantasies and we lose contact with the real lives and difficulties of our people.

97. Those who have fallen into this worldliness look on from above and afar, they reject the prophecy of their brothers and sisters, they discredit those who raise questions, they constantly point out the mistakes of others and they are obsessed by appearances. Their hearts are open only to the limited horizon of their own immanence and interests, and as a consequence they neither learn from

their sins nor are they genuinely open to forgiveness. This is a tremendous corruption disguised as a good. We need to avoid it by making the Church constantly go out from herself, keeping her mission focused on Jesus Christ, and her commitment to the poor. God save us from a worldly Church with superficial spiritual and pastoral trappings! This stifling worldliness can only be healed by breathing in the pure air of the Holy Spirit who frees us from self-centredness cloaked in an outward religiosity bereft of God. Let us not allow ourselves to be robbed of the Gospel!

No to Warring Among Ourselves

98. How many wars take place within the people of God and in our different communities! In our neighbourhoods and in the workplace, how many wars are caused by envy and jealousy, even among Christians! Spiritual worldliness leads some Christians to war with other Christians who stand in the way of their quest for power, prestige, pleasure and economic security. Some are even no longer content to live as part of the greater Church community but stoke a spirit of exclusivity, creating an "inner circle". Instead of belonging to the whole Church in all its rich variety, they belong to this or that group which thinks itself different or special.

99. Our world is being torn apart by wars and violence, and wounded by a widespread individualism which divides human beings, setting them against one another as they

pursue their own well-being. In various countries, conflicts and old divisions from the past are re-emerging. I especially ask Christians in communities throughout the world to offer a radiant and attractive witness of fraternal communion. Let everyone admire how you care for one another, and how you encourage and accompany one another: "By this everyone will know that you are my disciples, if you have love for one another" (Jn 13:35). This was Jesus' heartfelt prayer to the Father: "That they may all be one... in us... so that the world may believe" (Jn 17:21). Beware of the temptation of jealousy! We are all in the same boat and headed to the same port! Let us ask for the grace to rejoice in the gifts of each, which belong to all.

100. Those wounded by historical divisions find it difficult to accept our invitation to forgiveness and reconciliation, since they think that we are ignoring their pain or are asking them to give up their memory and ideals. But if they see the witness of authentically fraternal and reconciled communities, they will find that witness luminous and attractive. It always pains me greatly to discover how some Christian communities, and even consecrated persons, can tolerate different forms of enmity, division, calumny, defamation, vendetta, jealousy and the desire to impose certain ideas at all costs, even to persecutions which appear as veritable witch hunts. Whom are we going to evangelize if this is the way we act?

101. Let us ask the Lord to help us understand the law of love. How good it is to have this law! How much good it does us to love one another, in spite of everything. Yes, in spite of everything! Saint Paul's exhortation is directed to each of us: "Do not be overcome by evil, but overcome evil with good" (Rom 12:21). And again: "Let us not grow weary in doing what is right" (Gal 6:9). We all have our likes and dislikes, and perhaps at this very moment we are angry with someone. At least let us say to the Lord: "Lord, I am angry with this person, with that person. I pray to you for him and for her". To pray for a person with whom I am irritated is a beautiful step forward in love, and an act of evangelization. Let us do it today! Let us not allow ourselves to be robbed of the ideal of fraternal love!

Other Ecclesial Challenges

102. Lay people are, put simply, the vast majority of the people of God. The minority – ordained ministers – are at their service. There has been a growing awareness of the identity and mission of the laity in the Church. We can count on many lay persons, although still not nearly enough, who have a deeply-rooted sense of community and great fidelity to the tasks of charity, catechesis and the celebration of the faith. At the same time, a clear awareness of this responsibility of the laity, grounded in their baptism and confirmation, does not appear in the same way in all places. In some cases, it is because lay persons have not been given the formation needed to take on im-

portant responsibilities. In others, it is because in their particular Churches room has not been made for them to speak and to act, due to an excessive clericalism which keeps them away from decision-making. Even if many are now involved in the lay ministries, this involvement is not reflected in a greater penetration of Christian values in the social, political and economic sectors. It often remains tied to tasks within the Church, without a real commitment to applying the Gospel to the transformation of society. The formation of the laity and the evangelization of professional and intellectual life represent a significant pastoral challenge.

103. The Church acknowledges the indispensable contribution which women make to society through the sensitivity, intuition and other distinctive skill sets which they, more than men, tend to possess. I think, for example, of the special concern which women show to others, which finds a particular, even if not exclusive, expression in motherhood. I readily acknowledge that many women share pastoral responsibilities with priests, helping to guide people, families and groups and offering new contributions to theological reflection. But we need to create still broader opportunities for a more incisive female presence in the Church. Because "the feminine genius is needed in all expressions in the life of society, the presence of women must also be guaranteed in the workplace"[72] and in the various

---

72. Pontifical Council for Justice and Peace, *Compendium of the Social Doctrine of the Church*, 295.

other settings where important decisions are made, both in the Church and in social structures.

104. Demands that the legitimate rights of women be respected, based on the firm conviction that men and women are equal in dignity, present the Church with profound and challenging questions which cannot be lightly evaded. The reservation of the priesthood to males, as a sign of Christ the Spouse who gives himself in the Eucharist, is not a question open to discussion, but it can prove especially divisive if sacramental power is too closely identified with power in general. It must be remembered that when we speak of sacramental power "we are in the realm of function, not that of dignity or holiness".[73] The ministerial priesthood is one means employed by Jesus for the service of his people, yet our great dignity derives from baptism, which is accessible to all. The configuration of the priest to Christ the head – namely, as the principal source of grace – does not imply an exaltation which would set him above others. In the Church, functions "do not favour the superiority of some vis-à-vis the others".[74] Indeed, a woman, Mary, is more important than the bishops. Even when the function of ministerial priesthood is considered "hierarchi-

73. John Paul II, Post-Synodal Apostolic Exhortation *Christifideles Laici* (30 December 1988), 51: AAS 81 (1989), 413.

74. Congregation for the Doctrine of the Faith, Declaration *Inter Insigniores* on the Question of the Admission of Women to the Ministerial Priesthood (15 October 1976): AAS 68 (1977) 115, cited in John Paul II, Post-Synodal Apostolic Exhortation *Christifideles Laici* (30 December 1988), note 190: AAS 81 (1989), 493.

cal", it must be remembered that "it is totally ordered to the holiness of Christ's members".[75] Its key and axis is not power understood as domination, but the power to administer the sacrament of the Eucharist; this is the origin of its authority, which is always a service to God's people. This presents a great challenge for pastors and theologians, who are in a position to recognize more fully what this entails with regard to the possible role of women in decision-making in different areas of the Church's life.

105. Youth ministry, as traditionally organized, has also suffered the impact of social changes. Young people often fail to find responses to their concerns, needs, problems and hurts in the usual structures. As adults, we find it hard to listen patiently to them, to appreciate their concerns and demands, and to speak to them in a language they can understand. For the same reason, our efforts in the field of education do not produce the results expected. The rise and growth of associations and movements mostly made up of young people can be seen as the work of the Holy Spirit, who blazes new trails to meet their expectations and their search for a deep spirituality and a more real sense of belonging. There remains a need, however, to ensure that these associations actively participate in the Church's overall pastoral efforts.[76]

---

75. John Paul II, Apostolic Letter *Mulieris Dignitatem* (15 August 1988), 27: AAS 80 (1988), 1718.

76. Cf. *Propositio* 51.

106. Even if it is not always easy to approach young people, progress has been made in two areas: the awareness that the entire community is called to evangelize and educate the young, and the urgent need for the young to exercise greater leadership. We should recognize that despite the present crisis of commitment and communal relationships, many young people are making common cause before the problems of our world and are taking up various forms of activism and volunteer work. Some take part in the life of the Church as members of service groups and various missionary initiatives in their own dioceses and in other places. How beautiful it is to see that young people are "street preachers" (*callejeros de la fe*), joyfully bringing Jesus to every street, every town square and every corner of the earth!

107. Many places are experiencing a dearth of vocations to the priesthood and consecrated life. This is often due to a lack of contagious apostolic fervour in communities which results in a cooling of enthusiasm and attractiveness. Wherever there is life, fervour and a desire to bring Christ to others, genuine vocations will arise. Even in parishes where priests are not particularly committed or joyful, the fraternal life and fervour of the community can awaken in the young a desire to consecrate themselves completely to God and to the preaching of the Gospel. This is particularly true if such a living community prays insistently for vocations and courageously proposes to its young people the path of special consecration. On the other hand, despite

the scarcity of vocations, today we are increasingly aware of the need for a better process of selecting candidates to the priesthood. Seminaries cannot accept candidates on the basis of any motivation whatsoever, especially if those motivations have to do with affective insecurity or the pursuit of power, human glory or economic well-being.

108. As I mentioned above, I have not sought to offer a complete diagnosis, but I invite communities to complete and enrich these perspectives on the basis of their awareness of the challenges facing them and their neighbours. It is my hope that, in doing so, they will realize that whenever we attempt to read the signs of the times it is helpful to listen to young people and the elderly. Both represent a source of hope for every people. The elderly bring with them memory and the wisdom of experience, which warns us not to foolishly repeat our past mistakes. Young people call us to renewed and expansive hope, for they represent new directions for humanity and open us up to the future, lest we cling to a nostalgia for structures and customs which are no longer life-giving in today's world.

109. Challenges exist to be overcome! Let us be realists, but without losing our joy, our boldness and our hope-filled commitment. Let us not allow ourselves to be robbed of missionary vigour!

CHAPTER THREE

THE PROCLAMATION
OF THE GOSPEL

110. After having considered some of the challenges of the present, I would now like to speak of the task which bears upon us in every age and place, for "there can be no true evangelization without the explicit proclamation of Jesus as Lord", and without "the primacy of the proclamation of Jesus Christ in all evangelizing work".[77] Acknowledging the concerns of the Asian bishops, John Paul II told them that if the Church "is to fulfil its providential destiny, evangelization as the joyful, patient and progressive preaching of the saving death and resurrection of Jesus Christ must be your absolute priority."[78] These words hold true for all of us.

---

77. John Paul II, Post-Synodal Apostolic Exhortation *Ecclesia in Asia* (6 November 1999), 19: AAS 92 (2000), 478.

78. Ibid, 2: AAS 92 (2000), 451.

I. THE ENTIRE PEOPLE OF GOD PROCLAIMS THE GOSPEL

111. Evangelization is the task of the Church. The Church, as the agent of evangelization, is more than an organic and hierarchical institution; she is first and foremost a people advancing on its pilgrim way towards God. She is certainly a mystery rooted in the Trinity, yet she exists concretely in history as a people of pilgrims and evangelizers, transcending any institutional expression, however necessary. I would like to dwell briefly on this way of understanding the Church, whose ultimate foundation is in the free and gracious initiative of God.

A People for Everyone

112. The salvation which God offers us is the work of his mercy. No human efforts, however good they may be, can enable us to merit so great a gift. God, by his sheer grace, draws us to himself and makes us one with him.[79] He sends his Spirit into our hearts to make us his children, transforming us and enabling us to respond to his love by our lives. The Church is sent by Jesus Christ as the sacrament of the salvation offered by God.[80] Through her evangelizing activity, she cooperates as an instrument of that divine

---

79. Cf. *Propositio* 4.

80. Cf. Second Vatican Ecumenical Council, Dogmatic Constitution on the Church *Lumen Gentium*, 1.

grace which works unceasingly and inscrutably. Benedict XVI put it nicely at the beginning of the Synod's reflections: "It is important always to know that the first word, the true initiative, the true activity comes from God and only by inserting ourselves into the divine initiative, only begging for this divine initiative, shall we too be able to become – with him and in him – evangelizers".[81] This principle of the primacy of grace must be a beacon which constantly illuminates our reflections on evangelization.

113. The salvation which God has wrought, and the Church joyfully proclaims, is for everyone.[82] God has found a way to unite himself to every human being in every age. He has chosen to call them together as a people and not as isolated individuals.[83] No one is saved by himself or herself, individually, or by his or her own efforts. God attracts us by taking into account the complex interweaving of personal relationships entailed in the life of a human community. This people which God has chosen and called is the Church. Jesus did not tell the apostles to form an exclusive and elite group. He said: "Go and make disciples of all nations" (Mt 28:19). Saint Paul tells us in the people of God, in the Church, "there is neither Jew or

---

81. Meditation during the First General Congregation of the XIII Ordinary General Assembly of the Synod of Bishops (8 October 2012): AAS 104 (2012), 897.

82. Cf. Propositio 6; Second Vatican Ecumenical Council, Pastoral Constitution on the Church in the Modern World Gaudium et Spes, 22.

83. Cf. Second Vatican Ecumenical Council, Dogmatic Constitution on the Church Lumen Gentium, 9.

Greek... for you are all one in Christ Jesus" (Gal 3:28). To those who feel far from God and the Church, to all those who are fearful or indifferent, I would like to say this: the Lord, with great respect and love, is also calling you to be a part of his people!

114. Being Church means being God's people, in accordance with the great plan of his fatherly love. This means that we are to be God's leaven in the midst of humanity. It means proclaiming and bringing God's salvation into our world, which often goes astray and needs to be encouraged, given hope and strengthened on the way. The Church must be a place of mercy freely given, where everyone can feel welcomed, loved, forgiven and encouraged to live the good life of the Gospel.

A People of Many Faces

115. The People of God is incarnate in the peoples of the earth, each of which has its own culture. The concept of culture is valuable for grasping the various expressions of the Christian life present in God's people. It has to do with the lifestyle of a given society, the specific way in which its members relate to one another, to other creatures and to God. Understood in this way, culture embraces the totality of a people's life.[84] Each people in the course of its his-

---

84. Cf. Third General Conference of the Latin American and Caribbean Bishops, *Puebla Document*, 23 March 1979, Nos. 386-387.

tory develops its culture with legitimate autonomy.[85] This is due to the fact that the human person, "by nature stands completely in need of life in society"[86] and always exists in reference to society, finding there a concrete way of relating to reality. The human person is always situated in a culture: "nature and culture are intimately linked".[87] Grace supposes culture, and God's gift becomes flesh in the culture of those who receive it.

116. In these first two Christian millennia, countless peoples have received the grace of faith, brought it to flower in their daily lives and handed it on in the language of their own culture. Whenever a community receives the message of salvation, the Holy Spirit enriches its culture with the transforming power of the Gospel. The history of the Church shows that Christianity does not have simply one cultural expression, but rather, "remaining completely true to itself, with unswerving fidelity to the proclamation of the Gospel and the tradition of the Church, it will also reflect the different faces of the cultures and peoples in which it is received and takes root".[88][88] In the diversity of peoples who experience the gift of God, each in accordance with its own culture, the Church expresses her genu-

---

85. Cf. Second Vatican Ecumenical Council, Pastoral Constitution on the Church in the Modern World *Gaudium et Spes*, 36.

86. Ibid, 25.

87. Ibid, 53.

88. John Paul II, Apostolic Letter *Novo Millennio Ineunte* (6 January 2001), 40: AAS 93 (2001), 295.

ine catholicity and shows forth the "beauty of her varied face".[89] In the Christian customs of an evangelized people, the Holy Spirit adorns the Church, showing her new aspects of revelation and giving her a new face. Through inculturation, the Church "introduces peoples, together with their cultures, into her own community",[90] for "every culture offers positive values and forms which can enrich the way the Gospel is preached, understood and lived".[91] In this way, the Church takes up the values of different cultures and becomes *sponsa ornata monilibus suis*, "the bride bedecked with her jewels" (cf. Is 61:10)".[92]

117. When properly understood, cultural diversity is not a threat to Church unity. The Holy Spirit, sent by the Father and the Son, transforms our hearts and enables us to enter into the perfect communion of the blessed Trinity, where all things find their unity. He builds up the communion and harmony of the people of God. The same Spirit is that harmony, just as he is the bond of love between the Father and the Son.[93] It is he who brings forth a rich variety

---

89. Ibid.

90. John Paul II, Encyclical Letter *Redemptoris Missio* (7 December 1990), 52: AAS 83 (1991), 300; cf. Apostolic Exhortation Catechesi Tradendae (16 October 1979) 53: AAS 71 (1979), 1321.

91. John Paul II, Post-Synodal Apostolic Exhortation *Ecclesia in Oceania* (22 November 2001), 16: AAS 94 (2002), 383.

92. John Paul II, Post-Synodal Apostolic Exhortation *Ecclesia in Africa* (14 September 1995), 61: AAS 88 (1996), 39.

93. Saint Thomas Aquinas, S. Th. I, q. 39, a. 8 cons. 2: "Without the Holy Spirit who is the bond of both, one cannot understand the connecting

of gifts, while at the same time creating a unity which is never uniformity but a multifaceted and inviting harmony. Evangelization joyfully acknowledges these varied treasures which the Holy Spirit pours out upon the Church. We would not do justice to the logic of the incarnation if we thought of Christianity as monocultural and monotonous. While it is true that some cultures have been closely associated with the preaching of the Gospel and the development of Christian thought, the revealed message is not identified with any of them; its content is transcultural. Hence in the evangelization of new cultures, or cultures which have not received the Christian message, it is not essential to impose a specific cultural form, no matter how beautiful or ancient it may be, together with the Gospel. The message that we proclaim always has a certain cultural dress, but we in the Church can sometimes fall into a needless hallowing of our own culture, and thus show more fanaticism than true evangelizing zeal.

118. The Bishops of Oceania asked that the Church "develop an understanding and a presentation of the truth of Christ working from the traditions and cultures of the region" and invited "all missionaries to work in harmony with indigenous Christians so as to ensure that the faith and the life of the Church be expressed in legitimate forms

---

unity between the Father and the Son"; cf. I, q. 37, a. 1, ad 3.

appropriate for each culture".[94] We cannot demand that peoples of every continent, in expressing their Christian faith, imitate modes of expression which European nations developed at a particular moment of their history, because the faith cannot be constricted to the limits of understanding and expression of any one culture.[95] It is an indisputable fact that no single culture can exhaust the mystery of our redemption in Christ.

We are All Missionary Disciples

119. In all the baptized, from first to last, the sanctifying power of the Spirit is at work, impelling us to evangelization. The people of God is holy thanks to this anointing, which makes it infallible *in credendo*. This means that it does not err in faith, even though it may not find words to explain that faith. The Spirit guides it in truth and leads it to salvation.[96] As part of his mysterious love for humanity, God furnishes the totality of the faithful with an instinct of faith – *sensus fidei* – which helps them to discern what is truly of God. The presence of the Spirit gives Christians a certain connaturality with divine realities, and a wisdom which enables them to grasp those realities intuitively, even

---

94. John Paul II, Post-Synodal Apostolic Exhortation *Ecclesia in Oceania* (22 November 2001), 17: AAS 94 (2002), 385.

95. John Paul II, Post-Synodal Apostolic Exhortation *Ecclesia in Asia* (6 November 1999), 20: AAS 92 (2000), 478-482.

96. Cf. Second Vatican Ecumenical Council, Dogmatic Constitution on the Church *Lumen Gentium*, 12.

THE JOY OF THE GOSPEL | 97

when they lack the wherewithal to give them precise expression.

120. In virtue of their baptism, all the members of the People of God have become missionary disciples (cf. Mt 28:19). All the baptized, whatever their position in the Church or their level of instruction in the faith, are agents of evangelization, and it would be insufficient to envisage a plan of evangelization to be carried out by professionals while the rest of the faithful would simply be passive recipients. The new evangelization calls for personal involvement on the part of each of the baptized. Every Christian is challenged, here and now, to be actively engaged in evangelization; indeed, anyone who has truly experienced God's saving love does not need much time or lengthy training to go out and proclaim that love. Every Christian is a missionary to the extent that he or she has encountered the love of God in Christ Jesus: we no longer say that we are "disciples" and "missionaries", but rather that we are always "missionary disciples". If we are not convinced, let us look at those first disciples, who, immediately after encountering the gaze of Jesus, went forth to proclaim him joyfully: "We have found the Messiah!" (Jn 1:41). The Samaritan woman became a missionary immediately after speaking with Jesus and many Samaritans come to believe in him "because of the woman's testimony" (Jn 4:39). So too, Saint Paul, after his encounter with Jesus Christ, "immediately proclaimed Jesus" (Acts 9:20; cf. 22:6-21). So what are we waiting for?

121. Of course, all of us are called to mature in our work as evangelizers. We want to have better training, a deepening love and a clearer witness to the Gospel. In this sense, we ought to let others be constantly evangelizing us. But this does not mean that we should postpone the evangelizing mission; rather, each of us should find ways to communicate Jesus wherever we are. All of us are called to offer others an explicit witness to the saving love of the Lord, who despite our imperfections offers us his closeness, his word and his strength, and gives meaning to our lives. In your heart you know that it is not the same to live without him; what you have come to realize, what has helped you to live and given you hope, is what you also need to communicate to others. Our falling short of perfection should be no excuse; on the contrary, mission is a constant stimulus not to remain mired in mediocrity but to continue growing. The witness of faith that each Christian is called to offer leads us to say with Saint Paul: "Not that I have already obtained this, or am already perfect; but I press on to make it my own, because Christ Jesus has made me his own" (Phil 3:12-13).

The Evangelizing Power of Popular Piety

122. In the same way, we can see that the different peoples among whom the Gospel has been inculturated are active collective subjects or agents of evangelization. This is because each people is the creator of their own culture and the protagonist of their own history. Culture is a dynamic

reality which a people constantly recreates; each generation passes on a whole series of ways of approaching different existential situations to the next generation, which must in turn reformulate it as it confronts its own challenges. Being human means "being at the same time son and father of the culture to which one belongs".[97] Once the Gospel has been inculturated in a people, in their process of transmitting their culture they also transmit the faith in ever new forms; hence the importance of understanding evangelization as inculturation. Each portion of the people of God, by translating the gift of God into its own life and in accordance with its own genius, bears witness to the faith it has received and enriches it with new and eloquent expressions. One can say that "a people continuously evangelizes itself".[98] Herein lies the importance of popular piety, a true expression of the spontaneous missionary activity of the people of God. This is an ongoing and developing process, of which the Holy Spirit is the principal agent.[99]

123. Popular piety enables us to see how the faith, once received, becomes embodied in a culture and is constantly passed on. Once looked down upon, popular piety came

---

97. John Paul II, Encyclical Letter *Fides et Ratio* (14 September 1998), 71: AAS 91 (1999), 60.

98. Third General Conference of the Latin American and Caribbean Bishops, Puebla Document, 23 March 1979, 450; cf. Fifth General Conference of the Latin American and Caribbean Bishops, *Aparecida Document*, 29 June 2007, 264.

99. John Paul II, Post-Synodal Apostolic Exhortation *Ecclesia in Asia* (6 November 1999), 21: AAS 92 (2000), 482-484.

to be appreciated once more in the decades following the Council. In the Exhortation *Evangelii Nuntiandi*, Pope Paul VI gave a decisive impulse in this area. There he stated that popular piety "manifests a thirst for God which only the poor and the simple can know"[100] and that "it makes people capable of generosity and sacrifice even to the point of heroism, when it is a question of bearing witness to belief".[101] Closer to our own time, Benedict XVI, speaking about Latin America, pointed out that popular piety is "a precious treasure of the Catholic Church", in which "we see the soul of the Latin American peoples".[102]

124. The Aparecida Document describes the riches which the Holy Spirit pours forth in popular piety by his gratuitous initiative. On that beloved continent, where many Christians express their faith through popular piety, the bishops also refer to it as "popular spirituality" or "the people's mysticism".[103] It is truly "a spirituality incarnated in the culture of the lowly".[104] Nor is it devoid of content; rather it discovers and expresses that content more by way of symbols than by discursive reasoning, and in the act of faith greater accent is placed on *credere in Deum* than on

---

100. No. 48: AAS 68 (1976), 38.

101. Ibid.

102. Opening Address of the Fifth General Conference of the Latin American and Caribbean Bishops (13 May 2007), 1: AAS 90 (2007), 446.

103. Fifth General Conference of the Latin American and Caribbean Bishops, *Aparecida Document*, 29 June 2007, 262.

104. Ibid., 263.

credere Deum.[105] It is "a legitimate way of living the faith, a way of feeling part of the Church and a manner of being missionaries";[106] it brings with itself the grace of being a missionary, of coming out of oneself and setting out on pilgrimage: "Journeying together to shrines and taking part in other manifestations of popular piety, also by taking one's children or inviting others, is in itself an evangelizing gesture".[107] Let us not stifle or presume to control this missionary power!

125. To understand this reality we need to approach it with the gaze of the Good Shepherd, who seeks not to judge but to love. Only from the affective connaturality born of love can we appreciate the theological life present in the piety of Christian peoples, especially among their poor. I think of the steadfast faith of those mothers tending their sick children who, though perhaps barely familiar with the articles of the creed, cling to a rosary; or of all the hope poured into a candle lighted in a humble home with a prayer for help from Mary, or in the gaze of tender love directed to Christ crucified. No one who loves God's holy people will view these actions as the expression of a purely human search for the divine. They are the manifestation of a theological life nourished by the working of the Holy Spirit who has been poured into our hearts (cf. Rom 5:5).

---

105. Cf. Saint Thomas Aquinas, *S. Th.*, II-II, q. 2, a. 2.

106. Fifth General Conference of the Latin American and Caribbean Bishops, *Aparecida Document*, 29 June 2007, 264.

107. Ibid.

126. Underlying popular piety, as a fruit of the inculturated Gospel, is an active evangelizing power which we must not underestimate: to do so would be to fail to recognize the work of the Holy Spirit. Instead, we are called to promote and strengthen it, in order to deepen the never-ending process of inculturation. Expressions of popular piety have much to teach us; for those who are capable of reading them, they are a *locus theologicus* which demands our attention, especially at a time when we are looking to the new evangelization.

Person to Person

127. Today, as the Church seeks to experience a profound missionary renewal, there is a kind of preaching which falls to each of us as a daily responsibility. It has to do with bringing the Gospel to the people we meet, whether they be our neighbours or complete strangers. This is the informal preaching which takes place in the middle of a conversation, something along the lines of what a missionary does when visiting a home. Being a disciple means being constantly ready to bring the love of Jesus to others, and this can happen unexpectedly and in any place: on the street, in a city square, during work, on a journey.

128. In this preaching, which is always respectful and gentle, the first step is personal dialogue, when the other person speaks and shares his or her joys, hopes and concerns for loved ones, or so many other heartfelt needs. Only af-

terwards is it possible to bring up God's word, perhaps by reading a Bible verse or relating a story, but always keeping in mind the fundamental message: the personal love of God who became man, who gave himself up for us, who is living and who offers us his salvation and his friendship. This message has to be shared humbly as a testimony on the part of one who is always willing to learn, in the awareness that the message is so rich and so deep that it always exceeds our grasp. At times the message can be presented directly, at times by way of a personal witness or gesture, or in a way which the Holy Spirit may suggest in that particular situation. If it seems prudent and if the circumstances are right, this fraternal and missionary encounter could end with a brief prayer related to the concerns which the person may have expressed. In this way they will have an experience of being listened to and understood; they will know that their particular situation has been placed before God, and that God's word really speaks to their lives.

129. We should not think, however, that the Gospel message must always be communicated by fixed formulations learned by heart or by specific words which express an absolutely invariable content. This communication takes place in so many different ways that it would be impossible to describe or catalogue them all, and God's people, with all their many gestures and signs, are its collective subject. If the Gospel is embedded in a culture, the message is no longer transmitted solely from person to person. In countries where Christianity is a minority, then,

along with encouraging each of the baptized to proclaim the Gospel, particular Churches should actively promote at least preliminary forms of inculturation. The ultimate aim should be that the Gospel, as preached in categories proper to each culture, will create a new synthesis with that particular culture. This is always a slow process and at we can be overly fearful. But if we allow doubts and fears to dampen our courage, instead of being creative we will remain comfortable and make no progress whatsoever. In this case we will not take an active part in historical processes, but become mere onlookers as the Church gradually stagnates.

Charisms at the Service of a Communion which Evangelizes

130. The Holy Spirit also enriches the entire evangelizing Church with different charisms. These gifts are meant to renew and build up the Church.[108] They are not an inheritance, safely secured and entrusted to a small group for safekeeping; rather they are gifts of the Spirit integrated into the body of the Church, drawn to the centre which is Christ and then channelled into an evangelizing impulse. A sure sign of the authenticity of a charism is its ecclesial character, its ability to be integrated harmoniously into the life of God's holy and faithful people for the good of all.

---

108. Cf. Second Vatican Ecumenical Council, Dogmatic Constitution on the Church *Lumen Gentium*, 12.

Something truly new brought about by the Spirit need not overshadow other gifts and spiritualities in making itself felt. To the extent that a charism is better directed to the heart of the Gospel, its exercise will be more ecclesial. It is in communion, even when this proves painful, that a charism is seen to be authentic and mysteriously fruitful. On the basis of her response to this challenge, the Church can be a model of peace in our world.

131. Differences between persons and communities can sometimes prove uncomfortable, but the Holy Spirit, who is the source of that diversity, can bring forth something good from all things and turn it into an attractive means of evangelization. Diversity must always be reconciled by the help of the Holy Spirit; he alone can raise up diversity, plurality and multiplicity while at the same time bringing about unity. When we, for our part, aspire to diversity, we become self-enclosed, exclusive and divisive; similarly, whenever we attempt to create unity on the basis of our human calculations, we end up imposing a monolithic uniformity. This is not helpful for the Church's mission.

Culture, Thought and Education

132. Proclaiming the Gospel message to different cultures also involves proclaiming it to professional, scientific and academic circles. This means an encounter between faith, reason and the sciences with a view to developing new approaches and arguments on the issue of credibility,

a creative apologetics[109] which would encourage greater openness to the Gospel on the part of all. When certain categories of reason and the sciences are taken up into the proclamation of the message, these categories then become tools of evangelization; water is changed into wine. Whatever is taken up is not just redeemed, but becomes an instrument of the Spirit for enlightening and renewing the world.

133. It is not enough that evangelizers be concerned to reach each person, or that the Gospel be proclaimed to the cultures as a whole. A theology – and not simply a pastoral theology – which is in dialogue with other sciences and human experiences is most important for our discernment on how best to bring the Gospel message to different cultural contexts and groups.[110] The Church, in her commitment to evangelization, appreciates and encourages the charism of theologians and their scholarly efforts to advance dialogue with the world of cultures and sciences. I call on theologians to carry out this service as part of the Church's saving mission. In doing so, however, they must always remember that the Church and theology exist to evangelize, and not be content with a desk-bound theology.

134. Universities are outstanding environments for articulating and developing this evangelizing commitment in

---

109. Cf. *Propositio* 17.
110. Cf. *Propositio* 30.

an interdisciplinary and integrated way. Catholic schools, which always strive to join their work of education with the explicit proclamation of the Gospel, are a most valuable resource for the evangelization of culture, even in those countries and cities where hostile situations challenge us to greater creativity in our search for suitable methods.[111]

II. THE HOMILY

135. Let us now look at preaching within the liturgy, which calls for serious consideration by pastors. I will dwell in particular, and even somewhat meticulously, on the homily and its preparation, since so many concerns have been expressed about this important ministry, and we cannot simply ignore them. The homily is the touchstone for judging a pastor's closeness and ability to communicate to his people. We know that the faithful attach great importance to it, and that both they and their ordained ministers suffer because of homilies: the laity from having to listen to them and the clergy from having to preach them! It is sad that this is the case. The homily can actually be an intense and happy experience of the Spirit, a consoling encounter with God's word, a constant source of renewal and growth.

136. Let us renew our confidence in preaching, based on the conviction that it is God who seeks to reach out to

111. Cf. *Propositio* 27.

others through the preacher, and that he displays his power through human words. Saint Paul speaks forcefully about the need to preach, since the Lord desires to reach other people by means of our word (cf. Rom 10:14-17). By his words our Lord won over the hearts of the people; they came to hear him from all parts (cf. Mk 1:45); they were amazed at his teachings (cf. Mk 6:2), and they sensed that he spoke to them as one with authority (cf. Mk 1:27). By their words the apostles, whom Christ established "to be with him and to be sent out to preach" (Mk 3:14), brought all nations to the bosom of the Church (cf. Mt 16:15.20).

The Liturgical Context

137. It is worthy remembering that "the liturgical proclamation of the word of God, especially in the eucharistic assembly, is not so much a time for meditation and catechesis as a dialogue between God and his people, a dialogue in which the great deeds of salvation are proclaimed and the demands of the covenant are continually restated".[112] The homily has special importance due to its eucharistic context: it surpasses all forms of catechesis as the supreme moment in the dialogue between God and his people which lead up to sacramental communion. The homily takes up once more the dialogue which the Lord has already established with his people. The preacher must know the heart

---

112. John Paul II, Apostolic Letter *Dies Domini* (31 May 1998), 41: AAS 90 (1998), 738-739.

of his community, in order to realize where its desire for God is alive and ardent, as well as where that dialogue, once loving, has been thwarted and is now barren.

138. The homily cannot be a form of entertainment like those presented by the media, yet it does need to give life and meaning to the celebration. It is a distinctive genre, since it is preaching situated within the framework of a liturgical celebration; hence it should be brief and avoid taking on the semblance of a speech or a lecture. A preacher may be able to hold the attention of his listeners for a whole hour, but in this case his words become more important than the celebration of faith. If the homily goes on too long, it will affect two characteristic elements of the liturgical celebration: its balance and its rhythm. When preaching takes place within the context of the liturgy, it is part of the offering made to the Father and a mediation of the grace which Christ pours out during the celebration. This context demands that preaching should guide the assembly, and the preacher, to a life-changing communion with Christ in the Eucharist. This means that the words of the preacher must be measured, so that the Lord, more than his minister, will be the centre of attention.

A Mother's Conversation

139. We said that the people of God, by the constant inner working of the Holy Spirit, is constantly evangelizing itself. What are the implications of this principle for preach-

ers? It reminds us that the Church is a mother, and that she preaches in the same way that a mother speaks to her child, knowing that the child trusts that what she is teaching is for his or her benefit, for children know that they are loved. Moreover, a good mother can recognize everything that God is bringing about in her children, she listens to their concerns and learns from them. The spirit of love which reigns in a family guides both mother and child in their conversations; therein they teach and learn, experience correction and grow in appreciation of what is good. Something similar happens in a homily. The same Spirit who inspired the Gospels and who acts in the Church also inspires the preacher to hear the faith of the God's people and to find the right way to preach at each Eucharist. Christian preaching thus finds in the heart of people and their culture a source of living water, which helps the preacher to know what must be said and how to say it. Just as all of us like to be spoken to in our mother tongue, so too in the faith we like to be spoken to in our "mother culture," our native language (cf. 2 Macc 7:21, 27), and our heart is better disposed to listen. This language is a kind of music which inspires encouragement, strength and enthusiasm.

140. This setting, both maternal and ecclesial, in which the dialogue between the Lord and his people takes place, should be encouraged by the closeness of the preacher, the warmth of his tone of voice, the unpretentiousness of his manner of speaking, the joy of his gestures. Even if the

homily at times may be somewhat tedious, if this maternal and ecclesial spirit is present, it will always bear fruit, just as the tedious counsels of a mother bear fruit, in due time, in the hearts of her children.

141. One cannot but admire the resources that the Lord used to dialogue with his people, to reveal his mystery to all and to attract ordinary people by his lofty teachings and demands. I believe that the secret lies in the way Jesus looked at people, seeing beyond their weaknesses and failings: "Fear not little flock, for it is your Father's good pleasure to give you the kingdom" (Lk 12:32); Jesus preaches with that spirit. Full of joy in the Spirit, he blesses the Father who draws the little ones to him: "I thank you Father, Lord of heaven and earth, that you have hidden these things from the wise and understanding and revealed them to babes" (Lk 10:21). The Lord truly enjoys talking with his people; the preacher should strive to communicate that same enjoyment to his listeners.

Words which Set Hearts on Fire

142. Dialogue is much more than the communication of a truth. It arises from the enjoyment of speaking and it enriches those who express their love for one another through the medium of words. This is an enrichment which does not consist in objects but in persons who share themselves in dialogue. A preaching which would be purely moralistic or doctrinaire, or one which turns into a lecture on

biblical exegesis, detracts from this heart-to-heart communication which takes place in the homily and possesses a quasi-sacramental character: "Faith comes from what is heard, and what is heard comes by the preaching of Christ" (Rom 10:17). In the homily, truth goes hand in hand with beauty and goodness. Far from dealing with abstract truths or cold syllogisms, it communicates the beauty of the images used by the Lord to encourage the practise of good. The memory of the faithful, like that of Mary, should overflow with the wondrous things done by God. Their hearts, growing in hope from the joyful and practical exercise of the love which they have received, will sense that each word of Scripture is a gift before it is a demand.

143. The challenge of an inculturated preaching consists in proclaiming a synthesis, not ideas or detached values. Where your synthesis is, there lies your heart. The difference between enlightening people with a synthesis and doing so with detached ideas is like the difference between boredom and heartfelt fervour. The preacher has the wonderful but difficult task of joining loving hearts, the hearts of the Lord and his people. The dialogue between God and his people further strengthens the covenant between them and consolidates the bond of charity. In the course of the homily, the hearts of believers keep silence and allow God to speak. The Lord and his people speak to one another in a thousand ways directly, without intermediaries. But in the homily they want someone to serve as an instrument and to express their feelings in such a way that afterwards,

each one may chose how he or she will continue the conversation. The word is essentially a mediator and requires not just the two who dialogue but also an intermediary who presents it for what it is, out of the conviction that "what we preach is not ourselves, but Jesus Christ as Lord, with ourselves as your servants for Jesus' sake" (2 Cor 4:5).

144. To speak from the heart means that our hearts must not just be on fire, but also enlightened by the fullness of revelation and by the path travelled by God's word in the heart of the Church and our faithful people throughout history. This Christian identity, as the baptismal embrace which the Father gave us when we were little ones, makes us desire, as prodigal children – and favourite children in Mary – yet another embrace, that of the merciful Father who awaits us in glory. Helping our people to feel that they live in the midst of these two embraces is the difficult but beautiful task of one who preaches the Gospel.

III. PREPARING TO PREACH

145. Preparation for preaching is so important a task that a prolonged time of study, prayer, reflection and pastoral creativity should be devoted to it. With great affection I wish to stop for a moment and offer a method of preparing homilies. Some may find these suggestions self-evident, but I consider it helpful to offer them as a way of emphasizing the need to devote quality time to this precious

ministry. Some pastors argue that such preparation is not possible given the vast number of tasks which they must perform; nonetheless, I presume to ask that each week a sufficient portion of personal and community time be dedicated to this task, even if less time has to be given to other important activities. Trust in the Holy Spirit who is at work during the homily is not merely passive but active and creative. It demands that we offer ourselves and all our abilities as instruments (cf. Rom 12:1) which God can use. A preacher who does not prepare is not "spiritual"; he is dishonest and irresponsible with the gifts he has received.

Reverence for Truth

146. The first step, after calling upon the Holy Spirit in prayer, is to give our entire attention to the biblical text, which needs to be the basis of our preaching. Whenever we stop and attempt to understand the message of a particular text, we are practising "reverence for the truth".[113] This is the humility of heart which recognizes that the word is always beyond us, that "we are neither its masters or owners, but its guardians, heralds and servants".[114] This attitude of humble and awe-filled veneration of the word is expressed by taking the time to study it with the greatest care and a holy fear lest we distort it. To interpret a biblical text, we

---

113. Paul VI, Apostolic Exhortation *Evangelii Nuntiandi* (8 December 1975), 78: AAS 68 (1976), 71.

114. Ibid.

need to be patient, to put aside all other concerns, and to give it our time, interest and undivided attention. We must leave aside any other pressing concerns and create an environment of serene concentration. It is useless to attempt to read a biblical text if all we are looking for are quick, easy and immediate results. Preparation for preaching requires love. We only devote periods of quiet time to the things or the people whom we love; and here we are speaking of the God whom we love, a God who wishes to speak to us. Because of this love, we can take as much time as we need, like every true disciple: "Speak, Lord, for your servant is listening" (1 Sam 3:9).

147. First of all, we need to be sure that we understand the meaning of the words we read. I want to insist here on something which may seem obvious, but which is not always taken into account: the biblical text which we study is two or three thousand years old; its language is very different from that which we speak today. Even if we think we understand the words translated into our own language, this does not mean that we correctly understand what the sacred author wished to say. The different tools provided by literary analysis are well known: attention to words which are repeated or emphasized, recognition of the structure and specific movement of a text, consideration of the role played by the different characters, and so forth. But our own aim is not to understand every little detail of a text; our most important goal is to discover its principal message, the message which gives structure and unity to the

text. If the preacher does not make this effort, his preaching will quite likely have neither unity nor order; what he has to say will be a mere accumulation of various disjointed ideas incapable of inspiring others. The central message is what the author primarily wanted to communicate; this calls for recognizing not only the author's ideas but the effect which he wanted to produce. If a text was written to console, it should not be used to correct errors; if it was written as an exhortation, it should not be employed to teach doctrine; if it was written to teach something about God, it should not be used to expound various theological opinions; if it was written as a summons to praise or missionary outreach, let us not use it to talk about the latest news.

148. Certainly, to understand properly the meaning of the central message of a text we need to relate it to the teaching of the entire Bible as handed on by the Church. This is an important principle of biblical interpretation which recognizes that the Holy Spirit has inspired not just a part of the Bible, but the Bible as a whole, and that in some areas people have grown in their understanding of God's will on the basis of their personal experience. It also prevents erroneous or partial interpretations which would contradict other teachings of the same Scriptures. But it does not mean that we can weaken the distinct and specific emphasis of a text which we are called to preach. One of the defects of a tedious and ineffectual preaching is precisely its inability to transmit the intrinsic power of the text which has been proclaimed.

Personalizing the Word

149. The preacher "ought first of all to develop a great personal familiarity with the word of God. Knowledge of its linguistic or exegetical aspects, though certainly necessary, is not enough. He needs to approach the word with a docile and prayerful heart so that it may deeply penetrate his thoughts and feelings and bring about a new outlook in him".[115] It is good for us to renew our fervour each day and every Sunday as we prepare the homily, examining ourselves to see if we have grown in love for the word which we preach. Nor should we forget that "the greater or lesser degree of the holiness of the minister has a real effect on the proclamation of the word".[116] As Saint Paul says, "we speak, not to please men, but to please God who tests our hearts" (1 Th 2:4). If we have a lively desire to be the first to hear the word which we must preach, this will surely be communicated to God's faithful people, for "out of the abundance of the heart, the mouth speaks" (Mt 12:34). The Sunday readings will resonate in all their brilliance in the hearts of the faithful if they have first done so in the heart of their pastor.

150. Jesus was angered by those supposed teachers who demanded much of others, teaching God's word but without being enlightened by it: "They bind heavy burdens, hard

---

115. John Paul II, Post-Synodal Apostolic Exhortation *Pastores Dabo Vobis* (25 March 1992), 26: AAS 84 (1992), 698.

116. Ibid., 25: AAS 84 (1992), 696.

to bear, and lay them on the shoulders of others; but they themselves will not lift a finger to move them" (Mt 23:4). The apostle James exhorted: "Not many of you should become teachers, my brethren, for you know that we who teach shall be judged with greater strictness" (Jas 3:1). Whoever wants to preach must be the first to let the word of God move him deeply and become incarnate in his daily life. In this way preaching will consist in that activity, so intense and fruitful, which is "communicating to others what one has contemplated".[117] For all these reasons, before preparing what we will actually say when preaching, we need to let ourselves be penetrated by that word which will also penetrate others, for it is a living and active word, like a sword "which pierces to the division of soul and spirit, of joints and marrow, and discerns the thoughts and intentions of the heart" (Heb 4:12). This has great pastoral importance. Today too, people prefer to listen to witnesses: they "thirst for authenticity" and "call for evangelizers to speak of a God whom they themselves know and are familiar with, as if they were seeing him".[118]

151. We are not asked to be flawless, but to keep growing and wanting to grow as we advance along the path of the Gospel; our arms must never grow slack. What is essential is that the preacher be certain that God loves him, that Jesus Christ has saved him and that his love always has

---

117. Saint Thomas Aquinas, *S. Th.* II-II, q. 188, a. 6.

118. Paul VI, Apostolic Exhortation *Evangelii Nuntiandi* (8 December 1975), 76: AAS 68 (1976), 68.

the last word. Encountering such beauty, he will often feel that his life does not glorify God as it should, and he will sincerely desire to respond more fully to so great a love. Yet if he does not take time to hear God's word with an open heart, if he does not allow it to touch his life, to challenge him, to impel him, and if he does not devote time to pray with that word, then he will indeed be a false prophet, a fraud, a shallow impostor. But by acknowledging his poverty and desiring to grow in his commitment, he will always be able to abandon himself to Christ, saying in the words of Peter: "I have no silver and gold, but what I have I give you" (Acts 3:6). The Lord wants to make use of us as living, free and creative beings who let his word enter their own hearts before then passing it on to others. Christ's message must truly penetrate and possess the preacher, not just intellectually but in his entire being. The Holy Spirit, who inspired the word, "today, just as at the beginning of the Church, acts in every evangelizer who allows himself to be possessed and led by him. The Holy Spirit places on his lips the words which he could not find by himself".[119]

Spiritual Reading

152. There is one particular way of listening to what the Lord wishes to tell us in his word and of letting ourselves be transformed by the Spirit. It is what we call *lectio divina*. It consists of reading God's word in a moment of prayer

---

119. Ibid., 75: AAS 68 (1976), 65.

and allowing it to enlighten and renew us. This prayerful reading of the Bible is not something separate from the study undertaken by the preacher to ascertain the central message of the text; on the contrary, it should begin with that study and then go on to discern how that same message speaks to his own life. The spiritual reading of a text must start with its literal sense. Otherwise we can easily make the text say what we think is convenient, useful for confirming us in our previous decisions, suited to our own patterns of thought. Ultimately this would be tantamount to using something sacred for our own benefit and then passing on this confusion to God's people. We must never forget that sometimes "even Satan disguises himself as an angel of light" (2 Cor 11:14).

153. In the presence of God, during a recollected reading of the text, it is good to ask, for example: "Lord, what does this text say to me? What is it about my life that you want to change by this text? What troubles me about this text? Why am I not interested in this? Or perhaps: What do I find pleasant in this text? What is it about this word that moves me? What attracts me? Why does it attract me?" When we make an effort to listen to the Lord, temptations usually arise. One of them is simply to feel troubled or burdened, and to turn away. Another common temptation is to think about what the text means for other people, and so avoid applying it to our own life. It can also happen that we look for excuses to water down the clear meaning of the text. Or we can wonder if God is demanding too much of

us, asking for a decision which we are not yet prepared to make. This leads many people to stop taking pleasure in the encounter with God's word; but this would mean forgetting that no one is more patient than God our Father, that no one is more understanding and willing to wait. He always invites us to take a step forward, but does not demand a full response if we are not yet ready. He simply asks that we sincerely look at our life and present ourselves honestly before him, and that we be willing to continue to grow, asking from him what we ourselves cannot as yet achieve.

An Ear to the People

154. The preacher also needs to keep his ear to the people and to discover what it is that the faithful need to hear. A preacher has to contemplate the word, but he also has to contemplate his people. In this way he learns "of the aspirations, of riches and limitations, of ways of praying, of loving, of looking at life and the world, which distinguish this or that human gathering," while paying attention "to actual people, to using their language, their signs and symbols, to answering the questions they ask".[120] He needs to be able to link the message of a biblical text to a human situation, to an experience which cries out for the light of God's word. This interest has nothing to do with shrewdness or calculation; it is profoundly religious

---

120. Ibid ., 63: AAS 68 (1976), 53

and pastoral. Fundamentally it is a "spiritual sensitivity for reading God's message in events",[121] and this is much more than simply finding something interesting to say. What we are looking for is "what the Lord has to say in this or that particular circumstance".[122] Preparation for preaching thus becomes an exercise in evangelical discernment, wherein we strive to recognize – in the light of the Spirit – "a call which God causes to resound in the historical situation itself. In this situation, and also through it, God calls the believer".[123]

155. In this effort we may need but think of some ordinary human experience such as a joyful reunion, a moment of disappointment, the fear of being alone, compassion at the sufferings of others, uncertainty about the future, concern for a loved one, and so forth. But we need to develop a broad and profound sensitivity to what really affects other people's lives. Let us also keep in mind that we should never respond to questions that nobody asks. Nor is it fitting to talk about the latest news in order to awaken people's interest; we have television programmes for that. It is possible, however, to start with some fact or story so that God's word can forcefully resound in its call to conversion, worship, commitment to fraternity and service, and so forth. Yet there will always be some who readily listen

121. Ibid ., 43: AAS 68 (1976), 33

122. Ibid.

123. John Paul II, Post-Synodal Apostolic Exhortation *Pastores Dabo Vobis* (25 March 1992), 10: AAS 84 (1992), 672.

to a preacher's commentaries on current affairs, while not letting themselves be challenged.

Homiletic Resources

156. Some people think they can be good preachers because they know what ought to be said, but they pay no attention to how it should be said, that is, the concrete way of constructing a sermon. They complain when people do not listen to or appreciate them, but perhaps they have never taken the trouble to find the proper way of presenting their message. Let us remember that "the obvious importance of the content of evangelization must not overshadow the importance of its ways and means".[124] Concern for the way we preach is likewise a profoundly spiritual concern. It entails responding to the love of God by putting all our talents and creativity at the service of the mission which he has given us; at the same time, it shows a fine, active love of neighbour by refusing to offer others a product of poor quality. In the Bible, for example, we can find advice on how to prepare a homily so as to best to reach people: "Speak concisely, say much in few words" (Sir 32:8).

157. Simply using a few examples, let us recall some practical resources which can enrich our preaching and make it more attractive. One of the most important things is to learn how to use images in preaching, how to appeal to

---

124. Paul VI, Apostolic Exhortation *Evangelii Nuntiandi* (8 December 1975), 40: AAS 68 (1976), 31.

imagery. Sometimes examples are used to clarify a certain point, but these examples usually appeal only to the mind; images, on the other hand, help people better to appreciate and accept the message we wish to communicate. An attractive image makes the message seem familiar, close to home, practical and related to everyday life. A successful image can make people savour the message, awaken a desire and move the will towards the Gospel. A good homily, an old teacher once told me, should have "an idea, a sentiment, an image."

158. Paul VI said that "the faithful... expect much from preaching, and will greatly benefit from it, provided that it is simple, clear, direct, well-adapted".[125] Simplicity has to do with the language we use. It must be one that people understand, lest we risk speaking to a void. Preachers often use words learned during their studies and in specialized settings which are not part of the ordinary language of their hearers. These are words that are suitable in theology or catechesis, but whose meaning is incomprehensible to the majority of Christians. The greatest risk for a preacher is that he becomes so accustomed to his own language that he thinks that everyone else naturally understands and uses it. If we wish to adapt to people's language and to reach them with God's word, we need to share in their lives and pay loving attention to them. Simplicity and clarity are two different things. Our language may be simple but our

---

125. Ibid., 43: AAS 68 (1976), 33.

preaching not very clear. It can end up being incomprehensible because it is disorganized, lacks logical progression or tries to deal with too many things at one time. We need to ensure, then, that the homily has thematic unity, clear order and correlation between sentences, so that people can follow the preacher easily and grasp his line of argument.

159. Another feature of a good homily is that it is positive. It is not so much concerned with pointing out what shouldn't be done, but with suggesting what we can do better. In any case, if it does draw attention to something negative, it will also attempt to point to a positive and attractive value, lest it remain mired in complaints, laments, criticisms and reproaches. Positive preaching always offers hope, points to the future, does not leave us trapped in negativity. How good it is when priests, deacons and the laity gather periodically to discover resources which can make preaching more attractive!

IV. EVANGELIZATION AND THE DEEPER UNDERSTANDING OF THE *KERYGMA*

160. The Lord's missionary mandate includes a call to growth in faith: "Teach them to observe all that I have commanded you" (Mt 28:20). Hence it is clear that that the first proclamation also calls for ongoing formation and maturation. Evangelization aims at a process of growth which entails taking seriously each person and God's plan

for his or her life. All of us need to grow in Christ. Evangelization should stimulate a desire for this growth, so that each of us can say wholeheartedly: "It is no longer I who live, but Christ who lives in me" (Gal 2:20).

161. It would not be right to see this call to growth exclusively or primarily in terms of doctrinal formation. It has to do with "observing" all that the Lord has shown us as the way of responding to his love. Along with the virtues, this means above all the new commandment, the first and the greatest of the commandments, and the one that best identifies us as Christ's disciples: "This is my commandment, that you love one another as I have loved you" (Jn 15:12). Clearly, whenever the New Testament authors want to present the heart of the Christian moral message, they present the essential requirement of love for one's neighbour: "The one who loves *his neighbour* has fulfilled the whole law… therefore love of neighbour is the fulfilling of the law" (Rom 13:8, 10). These are the words of Saint Paul, for whom the commandment of love not only sums up the law but constitutes its very heart and purpose: "For the whole law is fulfilled in one word, 'you shall love your neighbour as yourself'" (Gal 5:14). To his communities Paul presents the Christian life as a journey of growth in love: "May the Lord make you increase and abound in love for one another and for all" (1 Th 3:12). Saint James likewise exhorts Christians to fulfil "the royal law according to the Scripture: You shall love your neighbour as yourself" (2:8), in order not to fall short of any commandment.

162. On the other hand this process of response and growth is always preceded by God's gift, since the Lord first says: "Baptize them in the name…" (Mt 28:19). The Father's free gift which makes us his sons and daughters, and the priority of the gift of his grace (cf. Eph 2:8-9; 1 Cor 4:7), enable that constant sanctification which pleases God and gives him glory. In this way, we allow ourselves to be transformed in Christ through a life lived "according to the Spirit" (Rom 8:5).

Kerygmatic and Mystagogical Catechesis

163. Education and catechesis are at the service of this growth. We already possess a number of magisterial documents and aids on catechesis issued by the Holy See and by various episcopates. I think in particular of the Apostolic Exhortation *Catechesi Tradendae* (1979), the *General Catechetical Directory* (1997) and other documents whose contents need not be repeated here. I would like to offer a few brief considerations which I believe to be of particular significance.

164. In catechesis too, we have rediscovered the fundamental role of the first announcement or kerygma, which needs to be the centre of all evangelizing activity and all efforts at Church renewal. The kerygma is trinitarian. The fire of the Spirit is given in the form of tongues and leads us to believe in Jesus Christ who, by his death and resurrection, reveals and communicates to us the Father's infinite mercy.

On the lips of the catechist the first proclamation must ring out over and over: "Jesus Christ loves you; he gave his life to save you; and now he is living at your side every day to enlighten, strengthen and free you." This first proclamation is called "first" not because it exists at the beginning and can then be forgotten or replaced by other more important things. It is first in a qualitative sense because it is the principal proclamation, the one which we must hear again and again in different ways, the one which we must announce one way or another throughout the process of catechesis, at every level and moment.[126] For this reason too, "the priest – like every other member of the Church – ought to grow in awareness that he himself is continually in need of being evangelized".[127]

165. We must not think that in catechesis the kerygma gives way to a supposedly more "solid" formation. Nothing is more solid, profound, secure, meaningful and wisdom-filled than that initial proclamation. All Christian formation consists of entering more deeply into the kerygma, which is reflected in and constantly illumines, the work of catechesis, thereby enabling us to understand more fully the significance of every subject which the latter treats. It is the message capable of responding to the desire for the infinite which abides in every human heart. The centrality of the kerygma calls for stressing those elements which

---

126. Cf. *Propositio* 9.

127. John Paul II, Post-Synodal Apostolic Exhortation *Pastores Dabo Vobis* (25 March 1992), 26: AAS 84 (1992), 698.

are most needed today: it has to express God's saving love which precedes any moral and religious obligation on our part; it should not impose the truth but appeal to freedom; it should be marked by joy, encouragement, liveliness and a harmonious balance which will not reduce preaching to a few doctrines which are at times more philosophical than evangelical. All this demands on the part of the evangelizer certain attitudes which foster openness to the message: approachability, readiness for dialogue, patience, a warmth and welcome which is non-judgmental.

166. Another aspect of catechesis which has developed in recent decades is mystagogic initiation.[128] This basically has to do with two things: a progressive experience of formation involving the entire community and a renewed appreciation of the liturgical signs of Christian initiation. Many manuals and programmes have not yet taken sufficiently into account the need for a mystagogical renewal, one which would assume very different forms based on each educational community's discernment. Catechesis is a proclamation of the word and is always centred on that word, yet it also demands a suitable environment and an attractive presentation, the use of eloquent symbols, insertion into a broader growth process and the integration of every dimension of the person within a communal journey of hearing and response.

---

128. Cf. *Propositio* 38.

167. Every form of catechesis would do well to attend to the "way of beauty" (*via pulchritudinis*).[129] Proclaiming Christ means showing that to believe in and to follow him is not only something right and true, but also something beautiful, capable of filling life with new splendour and profound joy, even in the midst of difficulties. Every expression of true beauty can thus be acknowledged as a path leading to an encounter with the Lord Jesus. This has nothing to do with fostering an aesthetic relativism[130] which would downplay the inseparable bond between truth, goodness and beauty, but rather a renewed esteem for beauty as a means of touching the human heart and enabling the truth and goodness of the Risen Christ to radiate within it. If, as Saint Augustine says, we love only that which is beautiful,[131] the incarnate Son, as the revelation of infinite beauty, is supremely lovable and draws us to himself with bonds of love. So a formation in the *via pulchritudinis* ought to be part of our effort to pass on the faith. Each particular Church should encourage the use of the arts in evangelization, building on the treasures of the past but also drawing upon the wide variety of contemporary expressions so as to transmit the faith in a new

---

129. Cf. *Propositio* 20.

130. Cf. Second Vatican Ecumenical Council, Decree on the Means of Social Communication *Inter Mirifica*, 6.

131. Cf. De Musica, VI, 13, 38: PL 32, 1183-1184; *Confessiones*, IV, 13.20: PL 32, 701.

"language of parables".[132] We must be bold enough to discover new signs and new symbols, new flesh to embody and communicate the word, and different forms of beauty which are valued in different cultural settings, including those unconventional modes of beauty which may mean little to the evangelizers, yet prove particularly attractive for others.

168. As for the moral component of catechesis, which promotes growth in fidelity to the Gospel way of life, it is helpful to stress again and again the attractiveness and the ideal of a life of wisdom, self-fulfilment and enrichment. In the light of that positive message, our rejection of the evils which endanger that life can be better understood. Rather than experts in dire predictions, dour judges bent on rooting out every threat and deviation, we should appear as joyful messengers of challenging proposals, guardians of the goodness and beauty which shine forth in a life of fidelity to the Gospel.

Personal Accompaniment in Processes of Growth

169. In a culture paradoxically suffering from anonymity and at the same time obsessed with the details of other people's lives, shamelessly given over to morbid curiosity, the Church must look more closely and sympatheti-

---

132. Benedict XVI, Address for the Screening of the Documentary *"Art and Faith" – Via Pulchritudinis* (25 October 2012): L'Osservatore Romano (27 October 2012), 7.

cally at others whenever necessary. In our world, ordained ministers and other pastoral workers can make present the fragrance of Christ's closeness and his personal gaze. The Church will have to initiate everyone – priests, religious and laity – into this "art of accompaniment" which teaches us to remove our sandals before the sacred ground of the other (cf. Ex 3:5). The pace of this accompaniment must be steady and reassuring, reflecting our closeness and our compassionate gaze which also heals, liberates and encourages growth in the Christian life.

170. Although it sounds obvious, spiritual accompaniment must lead others ever closer to God, in whom we attain true freedom. Some people think they are free if they can avoid God; they fail to see that they remain existentially orphaned, helpless, homeless. They cease being pilgrims and become drifters, flitting around themselves and never getting anywhere. To accompany them would be counterproductive if it became a sort of therapy supporting their self-absorption and ceased to be a pilgrimage with Christ to the Father.

171. Today more than ever we need men and women who, on the basis of their experience of accompanying others, are familiar with processes which call for prudence, understanding, patience and docility to the Spirit, so that they can protect the sheep from wolves who would scatter the flock. We need to practice the art of listening, which is more than simply hearing. Listening, in communication,

is an openness of heart which makes possible that close-ness without which genuine spiritual encounter cannot oc-cur. Listening helps us to find the right gesture and word which shows that we are more than simply bystanders. Only through such respectful and compassionate listening can we enter on the paths of true growth and awaken a yearning for the Christian ideal: the desire to respond fully to God's love and to bring to fruition what he has sown in our lives. But this always demands the patience of one who knows full well what Saint Thomas Aquinas tells us: that anyone can have grace and charity, and yet falter in the exercise of the virtues because of persistent "contrary inclinations".[133] In other words, the organic unity of the virtues always and necessarily exists *in habitu*, even though forms of conditioning can hinder the operations of those virtuous habits. Hence the need for "a pedagogy which will introduce people step by step to the full appropriation of the mystery".[134] Reaching a level of maturity where indi-viduals can make truly free and responsible decisions calls for much time and patience. As Blessed Peter Faber used to say: "Time is God's messenger".

172. One who accompanies others has to realize that each person's situation before God and their life in grace are mysteries which no one can fully know from without. The

---

133. S. Th., I-II, q. 65, a. 3, ad 2: "*propter aliquas dispositiones contrarias*".

134. John Paul II, Post-Synodal Apostolic Exhortation *Ecclesia in Asia* (6 November 1999), 20: AAS 92 (2000), 481.

Gospel tells us to correct others and to help them to grow on the basis of a recognition of the objective evil of their actions (cf. Mt 18:15), but without making judgments about their responsibility and culpability (cf. Mt 7:1; Lk 6:37). Someone good at such accompaniment does not give in to frustrations or fears. He or she invites others to let themselves be healed, to take up their mat, embrace the cross, leave all behind and go forth ever anew to proclaim the Gospel. Our personal experience of being accompanied and assisted, and of openness to those who accompany us, will teach us to be patient and compassionate with others, and to find the right way to gain their trust, their openness and their readiness to grow.

173. Genuine spiritual accompaniment always begins and flourishes in the context of service to the mission of evangelization. Paul's relationship with Timothy and Titus provides an example of this accompaniment and formation which takes place in the midst of apostolic activity. Entrusting them with the mission of remaining in each city to "put in order what remains to be done" (Tit 1:5; cf. 1 Tim 1:3-5), Paul also gives them rules for their personal lives and their pastoral activity. This is clearly distinct from every kind of intrusive accompaniment or isolated self-realization. Missionary disciples accompany missionary disciples.

Centred on the Word of God

174. Not only the homily has to be nourished by the word of God. All evangelization is based on that word, listened to, meditated upon, lived, celebrated and witnessed to. The sacred Scriptures are the very source of evangelization. Consequently, we need to be constantly trained in hearing the word. The Church does not evangelize unless she constantly lets herself be evangelized. It is indispensable that the word of God "be ever more fully at the heart of every ecclesial activity".[135] God's word, listened to and celebrated, above all in the Eucharist, nourishes and inwardly strengthens Christians, enabling them to offer an authentic witness to the Gospel in daily life. We have long since moved beyond that old contraposition between word and sacrament. The preaching of the word, living and effective, prepares for the reception of the sacrament, and in the sacrament that word attains its maximum efficacy.

175. The study of the sacred Scriptures must be a door opened to every believer.[136] It is essential that the revealed word radically enrich our catechesis and all our efforts to pass on the faith.[137] Evangelization demands familiarity with God's word, which calls for dioceses, parishes and

---

135. Benedict XVI , Post-Synodal Apostolic Exhortation *Verbum Domini* (30 September 2010), 1: AAS 102 (2010), 682.

136. Cf. *Propositio* 11.

137. Cf. Second Vatican Ecumenical Council, Dogmatic Constitution on Divine Revelation *Dei Verbum*, 21-22.

136 | POPE FRANCIS

Catholic associations to provide for a serious, ongoing study of the Bible, while encouraging its prayerful individual and communal reading.[138] We do not blindly seek God, or wait for him to speak to us first, for "God has already spoken, and there is nothing further that we need to know, which has not been revealed to us".[139] Let us receive the sublime treasure of the revealed word.

138. Cf. Benedict XVI, Post-Synodal Apostolic Exhortation *Verbum Domini* (30 September 2010), 86-87: AAS 102 (2010), 757-760.

139. Benedict XVI, Address during the First General Congregation of the Synod of Bishops (8 October 2012): AAS 104 (2012), 896.

CHAPTER FOUR

THE SOCIAL DIMENSION OF EVANGELIZATION

176. To evangelize is to make the kingdom of God present in our world. Yet "any partial or fragmentary definition which attempts to render the reality of evangelization in all its richness, complexity and dynamism does so only at the risk of impoverishing it and even of distorting it".140 I would now like to share my concerns about the social dimension of evangelization, precisely because if this dimension is not properly brought out, there is a constant risk of distorting the authentic and integral meaning of the mission of evangelization.

---

140. Paul VI, Post-Synodal Apostolic Exhortation *Evangelii Nuntiandi* (8 December 1975), 17: AAS 68 (1976), 17.

I. COMMUNAL AND SOCIETAL REPERCUSSIONS OF THE KERYGMA

177. The kerygma has a clear social content: at the very heart of the Gospel is life in community and engagement with others. The content of the first proclamation has an immediate moral implication centred on charity.

Confession of Faith and Commitment to Society

178. To believe in a Father who loves all men and women with an infinite love means realizing that "he thereby confers upon them an infinite dignity".[141] To believe that the Son of God assumed our human flesh means that each human person has been taken up into the very heart of God. To believe that Jesus shed his blood for us removes any doubt about the boundless love which ennobles each human being. Our redemption has a social dimension because "God, in Christ, redeems not only the individual person, but also the social relations existing between men".[142] To believe that the Holy Spirit is at work in everyone means realizing that he seeks to penetrate every human situation and all social bonds: "The Holy Spirit can be said to possess an infinite creativity, proper to the divine mind, which

---

141. John Paul II, *Message to the Handicapped, Angelus* (16 November 1980): *Insegnamenti*, 3/2 (1980), 1232.

142. Pontifical Council for Justice and Peace, *Compendium of the Social Doctrine of the Church*, 52.

knows how to loosen the knots of human affairs, even the most complex and inscrutable".[143] Evangelization is meant to cooperate with this liberating work of the Spirit. The very mystery of the Trinity reminds us that we have been created in the image of that divine communion, and so we cannot achieve fulfilment or salvation purely by our own efforts. From the heart of the Gospel we see the profound connection between evangelization and human advancement, which must necessarily find expression and develop in every work of evangelization. Accepting the first proclamation, which invites us to receive God's love and to love him in return with the very love which is his gift, brings forth in our lives and actions a primary and fundamental response: to desire, seek and protect the good of others.

179. This inseparable bond between our acceptance of the message of salvation and genuine fraternal love appears in several scriptural texts which we would do well to meditate upon, in order to appreciate all their consequences. The message is one which we often take for granted, and can repeat almost mechanically, without necessarily ensuring that it has a real effect on our lives and in our communities. How dangerous and harmful this is, for it makes us lose our amazement, our excitement and our zeal for living the Gospel of fraternity and justice! God's word teaches that our brothers and sisters are the prolongation of the incarnation for each of us: "As you did it to one of these,

---

143. John Paul, *Catechesis* (24 April 1991): *Insegnamenti*, 14/1 (1991), 853.

the least of my brethren, you did it to me" (Mt 25:40). The way we treat others has a transcendent dimension: "The measure you give will be the measure you get" (Mt 7:2). It corresponds to the mercy which God has shown us: "Be merciful, just as your Father is merciful. Do not judge, and you will not be judged; do not condemn, and you will not be condemned. Forgive, and you will be forgiven; give, and it will be given to you... For the measure you give will be the measure you get back" (Lk 6:36-38). What these passages make clear is the absolute priority of "going forth from ourselves towards our brothers and sisters" as one of the two great commandments which ground every moral norm and as the clearest sign for discerning spiritual growth in response to God's completely free gift. For this reason, "the service of charity is also a constituent element of the Church's mission and an indispensable expression of her very being".[144] By her very nature the Church is missionary; she abounds in effective charity and a compassion which understands, assists and promotes.

The Kingdom and its Challenge

180. Reading the Scriptures also makes it clear that the Gospel is not merely about our personal relationship with God. Nor should our loving response to God be seen simply as an accumulation of small personal gestures to indi-

---

144. Benedict XVI, Motu Proprio *Intima Ecclesiae Natura* (11 November 2012): AAS 104 (2012), 996.

viduals in need, a kind of "charity à la carte", or a series of acts aimed solely at easing our conscience. The Gospel is about the kingdom of God (cf. Lk 4:43); it is about loving God who reigns in our world. To the extent that he reigns within us, the life of society will be a setting for universal fraternity, justice, peace and dignity. Both Christian preaching and life, then, are meant to have an impact on society. We are seeking God's kingdom: "Seek first God's kingdom and his righteousness, and all these things will be given to you as well" (Mt 6:33). Jesus' mission is to inaugurate the kingdom of his Father; he commands his disciples to proclaim the good news that "the kingdom of heaven is at hand" (Mt 10:7).

181. The kingdom, already present and growing in our midst, engages us at every level of our being and reminds us of the principle of discernment which Pope Paul VI applied to true development: it must be directed to "all men and the whole man".[145] We know that "evangelization would not be complete if it did not take account of the unceasing interplay of the Gospel and of man's concrete life, both personal and social".[146] This is the principle of universality intrinsic to the Gospel, for the Father desires the salvation of every man and woman, and his saving plan consists in "gathering up all things in Christ, things

---

145. Encyclical Letter *Populorum Progressio* (16 March 1967), 14: AAS 59 (1967), 264.

146. Paul VI, Apostolic Exhortation *Evangelii Nuntiandi* (8 December 1975), 29: AAS 68 (1976), 25.

in heaven and things on earth" (Eph 1:10). Our mandate is to "go into all the world and proclaim the good news to the whole creation" (Mk 16:15), for "the creation waits with eager longing for the revealing of the children of God" (Rom 8:19). Here, "the creation" refers to every aspect of human life; consequently, "the mission of proclaiming the good news of Jesus Christ has a universal destination. Its mandate of charity encompasses all dimensions of existence, all individuals, all areas of community life, and all peoples. Nothing human can be alien to it".[147] True Christian hope, which seeks the eschatological kingdom, always generates history.

The Church's Teaching on Social Questions

182. The Church's teachings concerning contingent situations are subject to new and further developments and can be open to discussion, yet we cannot help but be concrete – without presuming to enter into details – lest the great social principles remain mere generalities which challenge no one. There is a need to draw practical conclusions, so that they "will have greater impact on the complexities of current situations".[148] The Church's pastors, taking into

---

147. Fifth General Conference of the Latin American and Caribbean Bishops, Aparecida Document, 29 June 2007, 380. Fifth General Conference of the Latin American and Caribbean Bishops, *Aparecida Document*, 29 June 2007, 380.

148. Pontifical Council for Justice and Peace, *Compendium of the Social Doctrine of the Church*, 9.

account the contributions of the different sciences, have the right to offer opinions on all that affects people's lives, since the task of evangelization implies and demands the integral promotion of each human being. It is no longer possible to claim that religion should be restricted to the private sphere and that it exists only to prepare souls for heaven. We know that God wants his children to be happy in this world too, even though they are called to fulfilment in eternity, for he has created all things "for our enjoyment" (1 Tim 6:17), the enjoyment of everyone. It follows that Christian conversion demands reviewing especially those areas and aspects of life "related to the social order and the pursuit of the common good".[149]

183. Consequently, no one can demand that religion should be relegated to the inner sanctum of personal life, without influence on societal and national life, without concern for the soundness of civil institutions, without a right to offer an opinion on events affecting society. Who would claim to lock up in a church and silence the message of Saint Francis of Assisi or Blessed Teresa of Calcutta? They themselves would have found this unacceptable. An authentic faith – which is never comfortable or completely personal – always involves a deep desire to change the world, to transmit values, to leave this earth somehow better that we found it. We love this magnificent planet

---

149. John Paul II, Post-Synodal Apostolic Exhortation *Ecclesia in America* (22 January 1999), 27: AAS 91 (1999), 762.

on which God has put us, and we love the human family which dwells here, with all its tragedies and struggles, its hopes and aspirations, its strengths and weaknesses. The earth is our common home and all of us are brothers and sisters. If indeed "the just ordering of society and of the state is a central responsibility of politics", the Church "cannot and must not remain on the sidelines in the fight for justice".[150] All Christians, their pastors included, are called to show concern for the building of a better world. This is essential, for the Church's social thought is primarily positive: it offers proposals, it works for change and in this sense it constantly points to the hope born of the loving heart of Jesus Christ. At the same time, it unites "its own commitment to that made in the social field by other Churches and Ecclesial Communities, whether at the level of doctrinal reflection or at the practical level".[151]

184. This is not the time or the place to examine in detail the many grave social questions affecting today's world, some of which I have dealt with in the second chapter. This Exhortation is not a social document, and for reflection on those different themes we have a most suitable tool in the Compendium of the Social Doctrine of the Church, whose use and study I heartily recommend. Furthermore, neither the Pope nor the Church have a monopoly on the

---

150. Benedict XVI, Encyclical Letter *Deus Caritas Est* (25 December 2005), 28: AAS 98 (2006), 239-240.

151. Pontifical Council for Justice and Peace, *Compendium of the Social Doctrine of the Church*, 12.

interpretation of social realities or the proposal of solutions to contemporary problems. Here I can repeat the insightful observation of Pope Paul VI: "In the face of such widely varying situations, it is difficult for us to utter a unified message and to put forward a solution which has universal validity. This is not our ambition, nor is it our mission. It is up to the Christian communities to analyze with objectivity the situation which is proper to their own country".[152]

185. In what follows I intend to concentrate on two great issues which strike me as fundamental at this time in history. I will treat them more fully because I believe that they will shape the future of humanity. These issues are first, the inclusion of the poor in society, and second, peace and social dialogue.

II. THE INCLUSION OF THE POOR IN SOCIETY

186. Our faith in Christ, who became poor, and was always close to the poor and the outcast, is the basis of our concern for the integral development of society's most neglected members.

---

152. Apostolic Letter *Octogesima Adveniens* (14 May 1971), 4: AAS 63 (1971), 403.

In Union with God, We Hear a Plea

187. Each individual Christian and every community is called to be an instrument of God for the liberation and promotion of the poor, and for enabling them to be fully a part of society. This demands that we be docile and attentive to the cry of the poor and to come to their aid. A mere glance at the Scriptures is enough to make us see how our gracious Father wants to hear the cry of the poor: "I have observed the misery of my people who are in Egypt; I have heard their cry on account of their taskmasters. Indeed, I know their sufferings, and I have come down to deliver them... so I will send you..." (Ex 3:7-8, 10). We also see how he is concerned for their needs: "When the Israelites cried out to the Lord, the Lord raised up for them a deliverer" (Jg 3:15). If we, who are God's means of hearing the poor, turn deaf ears to this plea, we oppose the Father's will and his plan; that poor person "might cry to the Lord against you, and you would incur guilt" (Dt 15:9). A lack of solidarity towards his or her needs will directly affect our relationship with God: "For if in bitterness of soul he calls down a curse upon you, his Creator will hear his prayer" (Sir 4:6). The old question always returns: "How does God's love abide in anyone who has the world's goods, and sees a brother or sister in need and yet refuses help?" (1 Jn 3:17). Let us recall also how bluntly the apostle James speaks of the cry of the oppressed: "The wages of the labourers who mowed your fields, which you kept back by

fraud, cry out, and the cries of the harvesters have reached the ears of the Lord of hosts" (5:4).

188. The Church has realized that the need to heed this plea is itself born of the liberating action of grace within each of us, and thus it is not a question of a mission reserved only to a few: "The Church, guided by the Gospel of mercy and by love for mankind, hears the cry for justice and intends to respond to it with all her might".[153] In this context we can understand Jesus' command to his disciples: "You yourselves give them something to eat!" (Mk 6:37): it means working to eliminate the structural causes of poverty and to promote the integral development of the poor, as well as small daily acts of solidarity in meeting the real needs which we encounter. The word "solidarity" is a little worn and at times poorly understood, but it refers to something more than a few sporadic acts of generosity. It presumes the creation of a new mindset which thinks in terms of community and the priority of the life of all over the appropriation of goods by a few.

189. Solidarity is a spontaneous reaction by those who recognize that the social function of property and the universal destination of goods are realities which come before private property. The private ownership of goods is justified by the need to protect and increase them, so that they can better serve the common good; for this reason, soli-

---

153. Congregation for the Doctrine of the Faith, Instruction *Libertatis Nuntius* (6 August 1984), XI, 1: AAS 76 (1984), 903.

darity must be lived as the decision to restore to the poor what belongs to them. These convictions and habits of solidarity, when they are put into practice, open the way to other structural transformations and make them possible. Changing structures without generating new convictions and attitudes will only ensure that those same structures will become, sooner or later, corrupt, oppressive and ineffectual.

190. Sometimes it is a matter of hearing the cry of entire peoples, the poorest peoples of the earth, since "peace is founded not only on respect for human rights, but also on respect for the rights of peoples".[154] Sadly, even human rights can be used as a justification for an inordinate defense of individual rights or the rights of the richer peoples. With due respect for the autonomy and culture of every nation, we must never forget that the planet belongs to all mankind and is meant for all mankind; the mere fact that some people are born in places with fewer resources or less development does not justify the fact that they are living with less dignity. It must be reiterated that "the more fortunate should renounce some of their rights so as to place their goods more generously at the service of others".[155] To speak properly of our own rights, we need to broaden our perspective and to hear the plea of other peoples and other

---

154. Pontifical Council for Justice and Peace, *Compendium of the Social Doctrine of the Church*, 157.

155. Paul VI, Apostolic Letter *Octogesima Adveniens* (14 May 1971), 23: AAS 63 (1971), 418.

regions than those of our own country. We need to grow in a solidarity which "would allow all peoples to become the artisans of their destiny",[156] since "every person is called to self-fulfilment".[157]

191. In all places and circumstances, Christians, with the help of their pastors, are called to hear the cry of the poor. This has been eloquently stated by the bishops of Brazil: "We wish to take up daily the joys and hopes, the difficulties and sorrows of the Brazilian people, especially of those living in the barrios and the countryside – landless, homeless, lacking food and health care – to the detriment of their rights. Seeing their poverty, hearing their cries and knowing their sufferings, we are scandalized because we know that there is enough food for everyone and that hunger is the result of a poor distribution of goods and income. The problem is made worse by the generalized practice of wastefulness".[158]

192. Yet we desire even more than this; our dream soars higher. We are not simply talking about ensuring nourishment or a "dignified sustenance" for all people, but also

---

156. Paul VI, Encyclical Letter *Populorum Progressio* (26 March 1967), 65: AAS 59 (1967), 289.

157. Ibid., 15: AAS 59 (1967), 265.

158. Conferência Nacional Dos Bispos Do Brazil, *Exigências evangélicas e éticas de superação da miséria e da fome*" (April 2002), Introduction, 2.

their "general temporal welfare and prosperity".[159] This means education, access to health care, and above all employment, for it is through free, creative,

participatory and mutually supportive labour that human beings express and enhance the dignity of their lives. A just wage enables them to have adequate access to all the other goods which are destined for our common use.

Fidelity to the Gospel, Lest we Run in Vain

193. We incarnate the duty of hearing the cry of the poor when we are deeply moved by the suffering of others. Let us listen to what God's word teaches us about mercy, and allow that word to resound in the life of the Church. The Gospel tells us: "Blessed are the merciful, because they shall obtain mercy" (Mt 5:7). The apostle James teaches that our mercy to others will vindicate us on the day of God's judgment: "So speak and so act as those who are to be judged under the law of liberty. For judgment is without mercy to one who has shown no mercy, yet mercy triumphs over judgment" (Jas 2:12-13). Here James is faithful to the finest tradition of post-exilic Jewish spirituality, which attributed a particular salutary value to mercy: "Break off your sins by practising righteousness, and your iniquities by showing mercy to the oppressed, that there may perhaps

---

159.. John XIII, Encyclical Letter *Mater et Magistra* (15 May 1961), 3: AAS 53 (1961), 402.

be a lengthening of your tranquillity" (Dan 4:27). The wisdom literature sees almsgiving as a concrete exercise of mercy towards those in need: "Almsgiving delivers from death, and it will purge away every sin" (Tob 12:9). The idea is expressed even more graphically by Sirach: "Water extinguishes blazing fire: so almsgiving atones for sin" (Sir 3:30). The same synthesis appears in the New Testament: "Maintain constant love for one another, for love covers a multitude of sins" (1 Pet 4:8). This truth greatly influenced the thinking of the Fathers of the Church and helped create a prophetic, counter-cultural resistance to the self-centred hedonism of paganism. We can recall a single example: "If we were in peril from fire, we would certainly run to water in order to extinguish the fire… in the same way, if a spark of sin flares up from our straw, and we are troubled on that account, whenever we have an opportunity to perform a work of mercy, we should rejoice, as if a fountain opened before so that the fire might be extinguished".[160]

194. This message is so clear and direct, so simple and eloquent, that no ecclesial interpretation has the right to relativize it. The Church's reflection on these texts ought not to obscure or weaken their force, but urge us to accept their exhortations with courage and zeal. Why complicate something so simple? Conceptual tools exist to heighten contact with the realities they seek to explain, not to distance us from them. This is especially the case with those

---

160. Saint Augustine, *De Catechizandis Rudibus*, I, XIX, 22: PL 40, 327.

biblical exhortations which summon us so forcefully to brotherly love, to humble and generous service, to justice and mercy towards the poor. Jesus taught us this way of looking at others by his words and his actions. So why cloud something so clear? We should not be concerned simply about falling into doctrinal error, but about remaining faithful to this light-filled path of life and wisdom. For "defenders of orthodoxy are sometimes accused of passivity, indulgence, or culpable complicity regarding the intolerable situations of injustice and the political regimes which prolong them".[161]

195. When Saint Paul approached the apostles in Jerusalem to discern whether he was "running or had run in vain" (Gal 2:2), the key criterion of authenticity which they presented was that he should not forget the poor (cf. Gal 2:10). This important principle, namely that the Pauline communities should not succumb to the self-centred lifestyle of the pagans, remains timely today, when a new self-centred paganism is growing. We may not always be able to reflect adequately the beauty of the Gospel, but there is one sign which we should never lack: the option for those who are least, those whom society discards.

196. Sometimes we prove hard of heart and mind; we are forgetful, distracted and carried away by the limitless possibilities for consumption and distraction offered by con-

---

161. Congregation for the Doctrine of the Faith, Instruction *Libertatis Nuntius* (6 August 1984), XI, 18: AAS 76 (1984), 907-908.

temporary society. This leads to a kind of alienation at every level, for "a society becomes alienated when its forms of social organization, production and consumption make it more difficult to offer the gift of self and to establish solidarity between people".[162]

The Special Place of the Poor in God's People

197. God's heart has a special place for the poor, so much so that he himself "became poor" (2 Cor 8:9). The entire history of our redemption is marked by the presence of the poor. Salvation came to us from the "yes" uttered by a lowly maiden from a small town on the fringes of a great empire. The Saviour was born in a manger, in the midst of animals, like children of poor families; he was presented at the Temple along with two turtledoves, the offering made by those who could not afford a lamb (cf. Lk 2:24; Lev 5:7); he was raised in a home of ordinary workers and worked with his own hands to earn his bread. When he began to preach the Kingdom, crowds of the dispossessed followed him, illustrating his words: "The Spirit of the Lord is upon me, because he has anointed me to preach good news to the poor" (Lk 4:18). He assured those burdened by sorrow and crushed by poverty that God has a special place for them in his heart: "Blessed are you poor, yours is the kingdom of God" (Lk 6:20); he made himself

---

162. John Paul II, Encyclical Letter *Centesimus Annus* (1 May 1991), 41: AAS 83 (1991), 844-845.

one of them: "I was hungry and you gave me food to eat", and he taught them that mercy towards all of these is the key to heaven (cf. Mt 25:5ff.).

198. For the Church, the option for the poor is primarily a theological category rather than a cultural, sociological, political or philosophical one. God shows the poor "his first mercy".[163] This divine preference has consequences for the faith life of all Christians, since we are called to have "this mind... which was in Jesus Christ" (Phil 2:5). Inspired by this, the Church has made an option for the poor which is understood as a "special form of primacy in the exercise of Christian charity, to which the whole tradition of the Church bears witness".[164] This option – as Benedict XVI has taught – "is implicit in our Christian faith in a God who became poor for us, so as to enrich us with his poverty".[165] This is why I want a Church which is poor and for the poor. They have much to teach us. Not only do they share in the *sensus fidei*, but in their difficulties they know the suffering Christ. We need to let ourselves be evangelized by them. The new evangelization is an invitation to acknowledge the saving power at work in their lives and to put them at the centre of the Church's pilgrim way.

---

163. John Paul II, Homily at Mass for the Evangelization of Peoples in Santo Domingo (11 October 1984), 5: AAS 77 (1985), 358.

164. John Paul II, Encyclical Letter *Sollicitudo Rei Socialis* (30 December 1987), 42: AAS 80 (1988), 572.

165. Address at the Inaugural Session of the Fifth General Conference of the Latin American and Caribbean Bishops (13 May 2007), 3: AAS 99 (2007), 450.

We are called to find Christ in them, to lend our voice to their causes, but also to be their friends, to listen to them, to speak for them and to embrace the mysterious wisdom which God wishes to share with us through them.

199. Our commitment does not consist exclusively in activities or programmes of promotion and assistance; what the Holy Spirit mobilizes is not an unruly activism, but above all an attentiveness which considers the other "in a certain sense as one with ourselves".[166] This loving attentiveness is the beginning of a true concern for their person which inspires me effectively to seek their good. This entails appreciating the poor in their goodness, in their experience of life, in their culture, and in their ways of living the faith. True love is always contemplative, and permits us to serve the other not out of necessity or vanity, but rather because he or she is beautiful above and beyond mere appearances: "The love by which we find the other pleasing leads us to offer him something freely".[167] The poor person, when loved, "is esteemed as of great value",[168] and this is what makes the authentic option for the poor differ from any other ideology, from any attempt to exploit the poor for one's own personal or political interest. Only on the basis of this real and sincere closeness can we properly accompany the poor on their path of liberation. Only

---

166. Saint Thomas Aquinas, *S. Th.*, II-II, q. 27, a. 2.

167. Ibid., I-II, q. 110, a. 1.

168. Ibid., I-II, q. 26, a. 3.

this will ensure that "in every Christian community the poor feel at home. Would not this approach be the greatest and most effective presentation of the good news of the kingdom?"[169] Without the preferential option for the poor, "the proclamation of the Gospel, which is itself the prime form of charity, risks being misunderstood or submerged by the ocean of words which daily engulfs us in today's society of mass communications".[170]

200. Since this Exhortation is addressed to members of the Catholic Church, I want to say, with regret, that the worst discrimination which the poor suffer is the lack of spiritual care. The great majority of the poor have a special openness to the faith; they need God and we must not fail to offer them his friendship, his blessing, his word, the celebration of the sacraments and a journey of growth and maturity in the faith. Our preferential option for the poor must mainly translate into a privileged and preferential religious care.

201. No one must say that they cannot be close to the poor because their own lifestyle demands more attention to other areas. This is an excuse commonly heard in academic, business or professional, and even ecclesial circles. While it is quite true that the essential vocation and mission of the lay faithful is to strive that earthly realities and all human activity may be transformed by the Gospel,[171] none of us

---

169. John Paul II, Apostolic Letter Novo *Millennio Ineunte* (6 January 2001), 50: AAS 93 (2001), 303.

170. Ibid.

171. Cf. *Propositio* 45.

can think we are exempt from concern for the poor and for social justice: "Spiritual conversion, the intensity of the love of God and neighbour, zeal for justice and peace, the Gospel meaning of the poor and of poverty, are required of everyone".[172] I fear that these words too may give rise to commentary or discussion with no real practical effect. That being said, I trust in the openness and readiness of all Christians, and I ask you to seek, as a community, creative ways of accepting this renewed call.

The Economy and the Distribution of Income

202. The need to resolve the structural causes of poverty cannot be delayed, not only for the pragmatic reason of its urgency for the good order of society, but because society needs to be cured of a sickness which is weakening and frustrating it, and which can only lead to new crises. Welfare projects, which meet certain urgent needs, should be considered merely temporary responses. As long as the problems of the poor are not radically resolved by rejecting the absolute autonomy of markets and financial speculation and by attacking the structural causes of inequality,[173] no solution will be found for the world's problems or, for

---

172. Congregation for the Doctrine of the Faith, Instruction *Libertatis Nuntius* (6 August 1984), XI, 18: AAS 76 (1984), 908.

173. This implies a commitment to "eliminate the structural causes of global economic dysfunction": Benedict XVI, *Address to the Diplomatic Corps* (8 January 2007): AAS 99 (2007), 73.

that matter, to any problems. Inequality is the root of social ills.

203. The dignity of each human person and the pursuit of the common good are concerns which ought to shape all economic policies. At times, however, they seem to be a mere addendum imported from without in order to fill out a political discourse lacking in perspectives or plans for true and integral development. How many words prove irksome to this system! It is irksome when the question of ethics is raised, when global solidarity is invoked, when the distribution of goods is mentioned, when reference in made to protecting labour and defending the dignity of the powerless, when allusion is made to a God who demands a commitment to justice. At other times these issues are exploited by a rhetoric which cheapens them. Casual indifference in the face of such questions empties our lives and our words of all meaning. Business is a vocation, and a noble vocation, provided that those engaged in it see themselves challenged by a greater meaning in life; this will enable them truly to serve the common good by striving to increase the goods of this world and to make them more accessible to all.

204. We can no longer trust in the unseen forces and the invisible hand of the market. Growth in justice requires more than economic growth, while presupposing such growth: it requires decisions, programmes, mechanisms and processes specifically geared to a better distribution of

income, the creation of sources of employment and an integral promotion of the poor which goes beyond a simple welfare mentality. I am far from proposing an irresponsible populism, but the economy can no longer turn to remedies that are a new poison, such as attempting to increase profits by reducing the work force and thereby adding to the ranks of the excluded.

205. I ask God to give us more politicians capable of sincere and effective dialogue aimed at healing the deepest roots – and not simply the appearances – of the evils in our world! Politics, though often denigrated, remains a lofty vocation and one of the highest forms of charity, inasmuch as it seeks the common good.[174] We need to be convinced that charity "is the principle not only of micro-relationships (with friends, with family members or within small groups) but also of macro-relationships (social, economic and political ones)".[175] I beg the Lord to grant us more politicians who are genuinely disturbed by the state of society, the people, the lives of the poor! It is vital that government leaders and financial leaders take heed and broaden their horizons, working to ensure that all citizens have dignified work, education and healthcare. Why not turn to God and ask him to inspire their plans? I am firmly convinced that openness to the transcendent can bring about a new

---

174. Cf. Commission Sociale de L'épiscopat Français, *Réhabiliter la politique* (17 February 1999); cf. PIUS XI, Message of 18 December 1927.

175. Benedict XVI, Encyclical Letter *Caritas in Veritate* (29 June 2009), 2: AAS 101 (2009), 642.

political and economic mindset which would help to break
down the wall of separation between the economy and the
common good of society.

206. Economy, as the very word indicates, should be the
art of achieving a fitting management of our common
home, which is the world as a whole. Each meaningful
economic decision made in one part of the world has re-
percussions everywhere else; consequently, no government
can act without regard for shared responsibility. Indeed, it
is becoming increasingly difficult to find local solutions for
enormous global problems which overwhelm local politics
with difficulties to resolve. If we really want to achieve a
healthy world economy, what is needed at this juncture of
history is a more efficient way of interacting which, with
due regard for the sovereignty of each nation, ensures the
economic well-being of all countries, not just of a few.

207. Any Church community, if it thinks it can comfort-
ably go its own way without creative concern and effective
cooperation in helping the poor to live with dignity and
reaching out to everyone, will also risk breaking down,
however much it may talk about social issues or criticize
governments. It will easily drift into a spiritual worldliness
camouflaged by religious practices, unproductive meetings
and empty talk.

208. If anyone feels offended by my words, I would respond that I speak them with affection and with the best

of intentions, quite apart from any personal interest or political ideology. My words are not those of a foe or an opponent. I am interested only in helping those who are in thrall to an individualistic, indifferent and self-centred mentality to be freed from those unworthy chains and to attain a way of living and thinking which is more humane, noble and fruitful, and which will bring dignity to their presence on this earth.

Concern for the Vulnerable

209. Jesus, the evangelizer par excellence and the Gospel in person, identifies especially with the little ones (cf. Mt 25:40). This reminds us Christians that we are called to care for the vulnerable of the earth. But the current model, with its emphasis on success and self-reliance, does not appear to favour an investment in efforts to help the slow, the weak or the less talented to find opportunities in life.

210. It is essential to draw near to new forms of poverty and vulnerability, in which we are called to recognize the suffering Christ, even if this appears to bring us no tangible and immediate benefits. I think of the homeless, the addicted, refugees, indigenous peoples, the elderly who are increasingly isolated and abandoned, and many others. Migrants present a particular challenge for me, since I am the pastor of a Church without frontiers, a Church which considers herself mother to all. For this reason, I exhort all countries to a generous openness which, rather than fear-

ing the loss of local identity, will prove capable of creating new forms of cultural synthesis. How beautiful are those cities which overcome paralysing mistrust, integrate those who are different and make this very integration a new factor of development! How attractive are those cities which, even in their architectural design, are full of spaces which connect, relate and favour the recognition of others!

211. I have always been distressed at the lot of those who are victims of various kinds of human trafficking. How I wish that all of us would hear God's cry: "Where is your brother?" (Gen 4:9). Where is your brother or sister who is enslaved? Where is the brother and sister whom you are killing each day in clandestine warehouses, in rings of prostitution, in children used for begging, in exploiting undocumented labour? Let us not look the other way. There is greater complicity than we think. The issue involves everyone! This infamous network of crime is now well established in our cities, and many people have blood on their hands as a result of their comfortable and silent complicity.

212. Doubly poor are those women who endure situations of exclusion, mistreatment and violence, since they are frequently less able to defend their rights. Even so, we constantly witness among them impressive examples of daily heroism in defending and protecting their vulnerable families.

213. Among the vulnerable for whom the Church wishes to care with particular love and concern are unborn children, the most defenceless and innocent among us. Nowadays efforts are made to deny them their human dignity and to do with them whatever one pleases, taking their lives and passing laws preventing anyone from standing in the way of this. Frequently, as a way of ridiculing the Church's effort to defend their lives, attempts are made to present her position as ideological, obscurantist and conservative. Yet this defence of unborn life is closely linked to the defence of each and every other human right. It involves the conviction that a human being is always sacred and inviolable, in any situation and at every stage of development. Human beings are ends in themselves and never a means of resolving other problems. Once this conviction disappears, so do solid and lasting foundations for the defence of human rights, which would always be subject to the passing whims of the powers that be. Reason alone is sufficient to recognize the inviolable value of each single human life, but if we also look at the issue from the standpoint of faith, "every violation of the personal dignity of the human being cries out in vengeance to God and is an offence against the creator of the individual".[176]

214. Precisely because this involves the internal consistency of our message about the value of the human person,

---

176. John Paul II, Post-Synodal Apostolic Exhortation *Christifideles Laici* (30 December 1988), 37: AAS 81 (1989), 461.

the Church cannot be expected to change her position on this question. I want to be completely honest in this regard. This is not something subject to alleged reforms or "modernizations". It is not "progressive" to try to resolve problems by eliminating a human life. On the other hand, it is also true that we have done little to adequately accompany women in very difficult situations, where abortion appears as a quick solution to their profound anguish, especially when the life developing within them is the result of rape or a situation of extreme poverty. Who can remain unmoved before such painful situations?

215. There are other weak and defenceless beings who are frequently at the mercy of economic interests or indiscriminate exploitation. I am speaking of creation as a whole. We human beings are not only the beneficiaries but also the stewards of other creatures. Thanks to our bodies, God has joined us so closely to the world around us that we can feel the desertification of the soil almost as a physical ailment, and the extinction of a species as a painful disfigurement. Let us not leave in our wake a swath of destruction and death which will affect our own lives and those of future generations.[177] Here I would make my own the touching and prophetic lament voiced some years ago by the bishops of the Philippines: "An incredible variety of insects lived in the forest and were busy with all kinds of tasks... Birds flew through the air, their bright plumes

---

177. Cf. *Propositio* 56.

and varying calls adding color and song to the green of the forests... God intended this land for us, his special creatures, but not so that we might destroy it and turn it into a wasteland... After a single night's rain, look at the chocolate brown rivers in your locality and remember that they are carrying the life blood of the land into the sea... How can fish swim in sewers like the Pasig and so many more rivers which we have polluted? Who has turned the wonderworld of the seas into underwater cemeteries bereft of color and life?"[178]

216. Small yet strong in the love of God, like Saint Francis of Assisi, all of us, as Christians, are called to watch over and protect the fragile world in which we live, and all its peoples.

III. THE COMMON GOOD AND PEACE IN SOCIETY

217. We have spoken at length about joy and love, but the word of God also speaks about the fruit of peace (cf. Gal 5:22).

218. Peace in society cannot be understood as pacification or the mere absence of violence resulting from the

---

178. Catholic Bishops Conference of the Philippines, Pastoral Letter *What is Happening to our Beautiful Land?* (29 January 1988).

domination of one part of society over others. Nor does true peace act as a pretext for justifying a social structure which silences or appeases the poor, so that the more affluent can placidly support their lifestyle while others have to make do as they can. Demands involving the distribution of wealth, concern for the poor and human rights cannot be suppressed under the guise of creating a consensus on paper or a transient peace for a contented minority. The dignity of the human person and the common good rank higher than the comfort of those who refuse to renounce their privileges. When these values are threatened, a prophetic voice must be raised.

219. Nor is peace "simply the absence of warfare, based on a precarious balance of power; it is fashioned by efforts directed day after day towards the establishment of the ordered universe willed by God, with a more perfect justice among men".[179] In the end, a peace which is not the result of integral development will be doomed; it will always spawn new conflicts and various forms of violence.

220. People in every nation enhance the social dimension of their lives by acting as committed and responsible citizens, not as a mob swayed by the powers that be. Let us not forget that "responsible citizenship is a virtue, and partici-

---

179. Paul VI, Encyclical Letter *Populorum Progressio* (26 March 1967), 76: AAS 59 (1967), 294-295.

pation in political life is a moral obligation".[180] Yet becoming a people demands something more. It is an ongoing process in which every new generation must take part: a slow and arduous effort calling for a desire for integration and a willingness to achieve this through the growth of a peaceful and multifaceted culture of encounter.

221. Progress in building a people in peace, justice and fraternity depends on four principles related to constant tensions present in every social reality. These derive from the pillars of the Church's social doctrine, which serve as "primary and fundamental parameters of reference for interpreting and evaluating social phenomena".[181] In their light I would now like to set forth these four specific principles which can guide the development of life in society and the building of a people where differences are harmonized within a shared pursuit. I do so out of the conviction that their application can be a genuine path to peace within each nation and in the entire world.

Time is Greater than Space

222. A constant tension exists between fullness and limitation. Fullness evokes the desire for complete possession, while limitation is a wall set before us. Broadly speaking,

---

180. United States Conference of Catholic Bishops, Pastoral Letter *Forming Conscience for Faithful Citizenship* (November 2007), 13.

181. Pontifical Council for Justice and Peace, *Compendium of the Social Doctrine of the Church*, 161.

"time" has to do with fullness as an expression of the horizon which constantly opens before us, while each individual moment has to do with limitation as an expression of enclosure. People live poised between each individual moment and the greater, brighter horizon of the utopian future as the final cause which draws us to itself. Here we see a first principle for progress in building a people: time is greater than space.

223. This principle enables us to work slowly but surely, without being obsessed with immediate results. It helps us patiently to endure difficult and adverse situations, or inevitable changes in our plans. It invites us to accept the tension between fullness and limitation, and to give a priority to time. One of the faults which we occasionally observe in sociopolitical activity is that spaces and power are preferred to time and processes. Giving priority to space means madly attempting to keep everything together in the present, trying to possess all the spaces of power and of self-assertion; it is to crystallize processes and presume to hold them back. Giving priority to time means being concerned about initiating processes rather than possessing spaces. Time governs spaces, illumines them and makes them links in a constantly expanding chain, with no possibility of return. What we need, then, is to give priority to actions which generate new processes in society and engage other persons and groups who can develop them to the point where they bear fruit in significant historical

events. Without anxiety, but with clear convictions and tenacity.

224. Sometimes I wonder if there are people in today's world who are really concerned about generating processes of people-building, as opposed to obtaining immediate results which yield easy, quick short-term political gains, but do not enhance human fullness. History will perhaps judge the latter with the criterion set forth by Romano Guardini: "The only measure for properly evaluating an age is to ask to what extent it fosters the development and attainment of a full and authentically meaningful human existence, in accordance with the peculiar character and the capacities of that age".[182]

225. This criterion also applies to evangelization, which calls for attention to the bigger picture, openness to suitable processes and concern for the long run. The Lord himself, during his earthly life, often warned his disciples that there were things they could not yet understand and that they would have to await the Holy Spirit (cf. Jn 16:12-13). The parable of the weeds among the wheat (cf. Mt 13:24-30) graphically illustrates an important aspect of evangelization: the enemy can intrude upon the kingdom and sow harm, but ultimately he is defeated by the goodness of the wheat.

---

182. *Das Ende der Neuzeit*, Würzburg, 1965, 30-31.

Unity Prevails Over Conflict

226. Conflict cannot be ignored or concealed. It has to be faced. But if we remain trapped in conflict, we lose our perspective, our horizons shrink and reality itself begins to fall apart. In the midst of conflict, we lose our sense of the profound unity of reality.

227. When conflict arises, some people simply look at it and go their way as if nothing happened; they wash their hands of it and get on with their lives. Others embrace it in such a way that they become its prisoners; they lose their bearings, project onto institutions their own confusion and dissatisfaction and thus make unity impossible. But there is also a third way, and it is the best way to deal with conflict. It is the willingness to face conflict head on, to resolve it and to make it a link in the chain of a new process. "Blessed are the peacemakers!" (Mt 5:9).

228. In this way it becomes possible to build communion amid disagreement, but this can only be achieved by those great persons who are willing to go beyond the surface of the conflict and to see others in their deepest dignity. This requires acknowledging a principle indispensable to the building of friendship in society: namely, that unity is greater than conflict. Solidarity, in its deepest and most challenging sense, thus becomes a way of making history in a life setting where conflicts, tensions and oppositions can achieve a diversified and life-giving unity. This is not to

opt for a kind of syncretism, or for the absorption of one into the other, but rather for a resolution which takes place on a higher plane and preserves what is valid and useful on both sides.

229. This principle, drawn from the Gospel, reminds us that Christ has made all things one in himself: heaven and earth, God and man, time and eternity, flesh and spirit, person and society. The sign of this unity and reconciliation of all things in him is peace. Christ "is our peace" (Eph 2:14). The Gospel message always begins with a greeting of peace, and peace at all times crowns and confirms the relations between the disciples. Peace is possible because the Lord has overcome the world and its constant conflict "by making peace through the blood of his cross" (Col 1:20). But if we look more closely at these biblical texts, we find that the locus of this reconciliation of differences is within ourselves, in our own lives, ever threatened as they are by fragmentation and breakdown.[183] If hearts are shattered in thousands of pieces, it is not easy to create authentic peace in society.

230. The message of peace is not about a negotiated settlement but rather the conviction that the unity brought by the Spirit can harmonize every diversity. It overcomes every conflict by creating a new and promising synthesis. Diversity is a beautiful thing when it can constantly enter

---

183. Cf. I. Quiles, S.J., *Filosofía de la educación personalista*, Buenos Aires, 1981, 46-53.

into a process of reconciliation and seal a sort of cultural covenant resulting in a "reconciled diversity". As the bishops of the Congo have put it: "Our ethnic diversity is our wealth... It is only in unity, through conversion of hearts and reconciliation, that we will be able to help our country to develop on all levels".[184]

Realities are More Important than Ideas

231. There also exists a constant tension between ideas and realities. Realities simply are, whereas ideas are worked out. There has to be continuous dialogue between the two, lest ideas become detached from realities. It is dangerous to dwell in the realm of words alone, of images and rhetoric. So a third principle comes into play: realities are greater than ideas. This calls for rejecting the various means of masking reality: angelic forms of purity, dictatorships of relativism, empty rhetoric, objectives more ideal than real, brands of ahistorical fundamentalism, ethical systems bereft of kindness, intellectual discourse bereft of wisdom.

232. Ideas – conceptual elaborations – are at the service of communication, understanding, and praxis. Ideas disconnected from realities give rise to ineffectual forms of idealism and nominalism, capable at most of classifying and defining, but certainly not calling to action. What calls us

---

184. Comité Permanent De La Conférence Épiscopale Nationale Du Congo, *Message sur la situation sécuritaire dans le pays* (5 December 2012), 11.

to action are realities illuminated by reason. Formal nominalism has to give way to harmonious objectivity. Otherwise, the truth is manipulated, cosmetics take the place
of real care for our bodies.[185] We have politicians – and
even religious leaders – who wonder why people do not
understand and follow them, since their proposals are so
clear and logical. Perhaps it is because they are stuck in the
realm of pure ideas and end up reducing politics or faith
to rhetoric. Others have left simplicity behind and have
imported a rationality foreign to most people.

233. Realities are greater than ideas. This principle has to
do with incarnation of the word and its being put into
practice: "By this you know the Spirit of God: every spirit
that confesses that Jesus Christ is come in the flesh is from
God" (1 Jn 4:2). The principle of reality, of a word already made flesh and constantly striving to take flesh anew,
is essential to evangelization. It helps us to see that the
Church's history is a history of salvation, to be mindful of
those saints who inculturated the Gospel in the life of our
peoples and to reap the fruits of the Church's rich bimil-
lennial tradition, without pretending to come up with a
system of thought detached from this treasury, as if we
wanted to reinvent the Gospel. At the same time, this principle impels us to put the word into practice, to perform
works of justice and charity which make that word fruitful.
Not to put the word into practice, not to make it reality, is

185. Cf. Plato, *Gorgias*, 465.

to build on sand, to remain in the realm of pure ideas and to end up in a lifeless and unfruitful self-centredness and gnosticism.

The Whole is Greater than the Part

234. An innate tension also exists between globalization and localization. We need to pay attention to the global so as to avoid narrowness and banality. Yet we also need to look to the local, which keeps our feet on the ground. Together, the two prevent us from falling into one of two extremes. In the first, people get caught up in an abstract, globalized universe, falling into step behind everyone else, admiring the glitter of other people's world, gaping and applauding at all the right times. At the other extreme, they turn into a museum of local folklore, a world apart, doomed to doing the same things over and over, and incapable of being challenged by novelty or appreciating the beauty which God bestows beyond their borders.

235. The whole is greater than the part, but it is also greater than the sum of its parts. There is no need, then, to be overly obsessed with limited and particular questions. We constantly have to broaden our horizons and see the greater good which will benefit us all. But this has to be done without evasion or uprooting. We need to sink our roots deeper into the fertile soil and history of our native place, which is a gift of God. We can work on a small scale, in our own neighbourhood, but with a larger perspective. Nor do

people who wholeheartedly enter into the life of a community need to lose their individualism or hide their identity; instead, they receive new impulses to personal growth. The global need not stifle, nor the particular prove barren.

236. Here our model is not the sphere, which is no greater than its parts, where every point is equidistant from the centre, and there are no differences between them. Instead, it is the polyhedron, which reflects the convergence of all its parts, each of which preserves its distinctiveness. Pastoral and political activity alike seek to gather in this polyhedron the best of each. There is a place for the poor and their culture, their aspirations and their potential. Even people who can be considered dubious on account of their errors have something to offer which must not be overlooked. It is the convergence of peoples who, within the universal order, maintain their own individuality; it is the sum total of persons within a society which pursues the common good, which truly has a place for everyone.

237. To Christians, this principle also evokes the totality or integrity of the Gospel which the Church passes down to us and sends us forth to proclaim. Its fullness and richness embrace scholars and workers, businessmen and artists, in a word, everyone. The genius of each people receives in its own way the entire Gospel and embodies it in expressions of prayer, fraternity, justice, struggle and celebration. The good news is the joy of the Father who desires that none of his little ones be lost, the joy of the Good Shepherd

who finds the lost sheep and brings it back to the flock. The Gospel is the leaven which causes the dough to rise and the city on the hill whose light illumines all peoples. The Gospel has an intrinsic principle of totality: it will always remain good news until it has been proclaimed to all people, until it has healed and strengthened every aspect of humanity, until it has brought all men and women together at table in God's kingdom. The whole is greater than the part.

IV. SOCIAL DIALOGUE AS A CONTRIBUTION TO PEACE

238. Evangelization also involves the path of dialogue. For the Church today, three areas of dialogue stand out where she needs to be present in order to promote full human development and to pursue the common good: dialogue with states, dialogue with society – including dialogue with cultures and the sciences – and dialogue with other believers who are not part of the Catholic Church. In each case, "the Church speaks from the light which faith offers",[186] contributing her two thousand year experience and keeping ever in mind the life and sufferings of human beings. This light transcends human reason, yet it can also prove meaningful and enriching to those who are not believers and it stimulates reason to broaden its perspectives.

---

186. Benedict XVI, Address to the Roman Curia (21 December 2012): AAS 105 (2013), 51.

239. The Church proclaims "the Gospel of peace" (Eph 6:15) and she wishes to cooperate with all national and international authorities in safeguarding this immense universal good. By preaching Jesus Christ, who is himself peace (cf. Eph 2:14), the new evangelization calls on every baptized person to be a peacemaker and a credible witness to a reconciled life.[187] In a culture which privileges dialogue as a form of encounter, it is time to devise a means for building consensus and agreement while seeking the goal of a just, responsive and inclusive society. The principal author, the historic subject of this process, is the people as a whole and their culture, and not a single class, minority, group or elite. We do not need plans drawn up by a few for the few, or an enlightened or outspoken minority which claims to speak for everyone. It is about agreeing to live together, a social and cultural pact.

240. It is the responsibility of the State to safeguard and promote the common good of society.[188] Based on the principles of subsidiarity and solidarity, and fully committed to political dialogue and consensus building, it plays a fundamental role, one which cannot be delegated, in working for the integral development of all. This role, at present, calls for profound social humility.

---

187. Cf. *Propositio* 14.

188. Cf. Catechism of the Catholic Church, 1910; Pontifical Council for Justice and Peace, *Compendium of the Social Doctrine of the Church*, 168.

241. In her dialogue with the State and with society, the Church does not have solutions for every particular issue. Together with the various sectors of society, she supports those programmes which best respond to the dignity of each person and the common good. In doing this, she proposes in a clear way the fundamental values of human life and convictions which can then find expression in political activity.

Dialogue Between Faith, Reason and Science

242. Dialogue between science and faith also belongs to the work of evangelization at the service of peace.[189] Whereas positivism and scientism "refuse to admit the validity of forms of knowledge other than those of the positive sciences",[190] the Church proposes another path, which calls for a synthesis between the responsible use of methods proper to the empirical sciences and other areas of knowledge such as philosophy, theology, as well as faith itself, which elevates us to the mystery transcending nature and human intelligence. Faith is not fearful of reason; on the contrary, it seeks and trusts reason, since "the light of reason and the light of faith both come from God"[191] and

---

189. Cf. *Propositio* 54.

190. John Paul II, *Encyclical Letter Fides et Ratio* (14 September 1998), 88: AAS 91 (1999), 74.

191. Saint Thomas Aquinas, Summa contra Gentiles, I, 7; cf. John Paul II, Encyclical Letter *Fides et Ratio* (14 September 1998), 43: AAS 91 (1999), 39.

cannot contradict each other. Evangelization is attentive to scientific advances and wishes to shed on them the light of faith and the natural law so that they will remain respectful of the centrality and supreme value of the human person at every stage of life. All of society can be enriched thanks to this dialogue, which opens up new horizons for thought and expands the possibilities of reason. This too is a path of harmony and peace.

243. The Church has no wish to hold back the marvellous progress of science. On the contrary, she rejoices and even delights in acknowledging the enormous potential that God has given to the human mind. Whenever the sciences – rigorously focused on their specific field of inquiry – arrive at a conclusion which reason cannot refute, faith does not contradict it. Neither can believers claim that a scientific opinion which is attractive but not sufficiently verified has the same weight as a dogma of faith. At times some scientists have exceeded the limits of their scientific competence by making certain statements or claims. But here the problem is not with reason itself, but with the promotion of a particular ideology which blocks the path to authentic, serene and productive dialogue.

Ecumenical Dialogue

244. Commitment to ecumenism responds to the prayer of the Lord Jesus that "they may all be one" (Jn 17:21). The credibility of the Christian message would be much

greater if Christians could overcome their divisions and the Church could realize "the fullness of catholicity proper to her in those of her children who, though joined to her by baptism, are yet separated from full communion with her".[192] We must never forget that we are pilgrims journeying alongside one another. This means that we must have sincere trust in our fellow pilgrims, putting aside all suspicion or mistrust, and turn our gaze to what we are all seeking: the radiant peace of God's face. Trusting others is an art and peace is an art. Jesus told us: "Blessed are the peacemakers" (Mt 5:9). In taking up this task, also among ourselves, we fulfil the ancient prophecy: "They shall beat their swords into ploughshares" (Is 2:4).

245. In this perspective, ecumenism can be seen as a contribution to the unity of the human family. At the Synod, the presence of the Patriarch of Constantinople, His Holiness Bartholomaios I, and the Archbishop of Canterbury, His Grace Rowan Williams, was a true gift from God and a precious Christian witness.[193]

246. Given the seriousness of the counter-witness of division among Christians, particularly in Asia and Africa, the search for paths to unity becomes all the more urgent. Missionaries on those continents often mention the criticisms, complaints and ridicule to which the scandal of divided Christians gives rise. If we concentrate on the con-

---

192. Second Vatican Council, Decree on *Ecumenism Unitatis Redintegratio*, 4.

193. Cf. *Propositio* 52.

victions we share, and if we keep in mind the principle of the hierarchy of truths, we will be able to progress decidedly towards common expressions of proclamation, service and witness. The immense numbers of people who have not received the Gospel of Jesus Christ cannot leave us indifferent. Consequently, commitment to a unity which helps them to accept Jesus Christ can no longer be a matter of mere diplomacy or forced compliance, but rather an indispensable path to evangelization. Signs of division between Christians in countries ravaged by violence add further causes of conflict on the part of those who should instead be a leaven of peace. How many important things unite us! If we really believe in the abundantly free working of the Holy Spirit, we can learn so much from one another! It is not just about being better informed about others, but rather about reaping what the Spirit has sown in them, which is also meant to be a gift for us. To give but one example, in the dialogue with our Orthodox brothers and sisters, we Catholics have the opportunity to learn more about the meaning of episcopal collegiality and their experience of synodality. Through an exchange of gifts, the Spirit can lead us ever more fully into truth and goodness.

Relations with Judaism

247. We hold the Jewish people in special regard because their covenant with God has never been revoked, for "the gifts and the call of God are irrevocable" (Rom 11:29). The Church, which shares with Jews an important part of the

sacred Scriptures, looks upon the people of the covenant and their faith as one of the sacred roots of her own Christian identity (cf. Rom 11:16-18). As Christians, we cannot consider Judaism as a foreign religion; nor do we include the Jews among those called to turn from idols and to serve the true God (cf. 1 Thes 1:9). With them, we believe in the one God who acts in history, and with them we accept his revealed word.

248. Dialogue and friendship with the children of Israel are part of the life of Jesus' disciples. The friendship which has grown between us makes us bitterly and sincerely regret the terrible persecutions which they have endured, and continue to endure, especially those that have involved Christians.

249. God continues to work among the people of the Old Covenant and to bring forth treasures of wisdom which flow from their encounter with his word. For this reason, the Church also is enriched when she receives the values of Judaism. While it is true that certain Christian beliefs are unacceptable to Judaism, and that the Church cannot refrain from proclaiming Jesus as Lord and Messiah, there exists as well a rich complementarity which allows us to read the texts of the Hebrew Scriptures together and to help one another to mine the riches of God's word. We can also share many ethical convictions and a common concern for justice and the development of peoples.

Interreligious Dialogue

250. An attitude of openness in truth and in love must characterize the dialogue with the followers of non-Christian religions, in spite of various obstacles and difficulties, especially forms of fundamentalism on both sides. Interreligious dialogue is a necessary condition for peace in the world, and so it is a duty for Christians as well as other religious communities. This dialogue is in first place a conversation about human existence or simply, as the bishops of India have put it, a matter of "being open to them, sharing their joys and sorrows".[194]In this way we learn to accept others and their different ways of living, thinking and speaking. We can then join one another in taking up the duty of serving justice and peace, which should become a basic principle of all our exchanges. A dialogue which seeks social peace and justice is in itself, beyond all merely practical considerations, an ethical commitment which brings about a new social situation. Efforts made in dealing with a specific theme can become a process in which, by mutual listening, both parts can be purified and enriched. These efforts, therefore, can also express love for truth.

251. In this dialogue, ever friendly and sincere, attention must always be paid to the essential bond between dialogue and proclamation, which leads the Church to main-

---

194. Indian Bishops' Conference, Final Declaration of the XXX Assembly: *The Role of the Church for a Better India* (8 March 2013), 8.9.

tain and intensify her relationship with non-Christians.[195] A facile syncretism would ultimately be a totalitarian gesture on the part of those who would ignore greater values of which they are not the masters. True openness involves remaining steadfast in one's deepest convictions, clear and joyful in one's own identity, while at the same time being "open to understanding those of the other party" and "knowing that dialogue can enrich each side".[196] What is not helpful is a diplomatic openness which says "yes" to everything in order to avoid problems, for this would be a way of deceiving others and denying them the good which we have been given to share generously with others. Evangelization and interreligious dialogue, far from being opposed, mutually support and nourish one another.[197]

252. Our relationship with the followers of Islam has taken on great importance, since they are now significantly present in many traditionally Christian countries, where they can freely worship and become fully a part of society. We must never forget that they "profess to hold the faith of Abraham, and together with us they adore the one, merciful God, who will judge humanity on the last day".[198]

---

195. Cf. *Propositio* 53.

196. John Paul II, Encyclical Letter *Redemptoris Missio* (7 December 1990), 56: AAS 83 (1991), 304.

197. Cf. Benedict XVI, Address to the Roman Curia (21 December 2012): AAS 105 (2006), 51; Second Vatican Ecumenical Council, Decree on the Missionary Activity of the Church Ad Gentes, 9; *Catechism of the Catholic Church*, 856.

198. Second Vatican Ecumenical Council, Dogmatic Constitution on the Church *Lumen Gentium*, 16.

The sacred writings of Islam have retained some Christian teachings; Jesus and Mary receive profound veneration and it is admirable to see how Muslims both young and old, men and women, make time for daily prayer and faithfully take part in religious services. Many of them also have a deep conviction that their life, in its entirety, is from God and for God. They also acknowledge the need to respond to God with an ethical commitment and with mercy towards those most in need.

253. In order to sustain dialogue with Islam, suitable training is essential for all involved, not only so that they can be solidly and joyfully grounded in their own identity, but so that they can also acknowledge the values of others, appreciate the concerns underlying their demands and shed light on shared beliefs. We Christians should embrace with affection and respect Muslim immigrants to our countries in the same way that we hope and ask to be received and respected in countries of Islamic tradition. I ask and I humbly entreat those countries to grant Christians freedom to worship and to practice their faith, in light of the freedom which followers of Islam enjoy in Western countries! Faced with disconcerting episodes of violent fundamentalism, our respect for true followers of Islam should lead us to avoid hateful generalisations, for authentic Islam and the proper reading of the Koran are opposed to every form of violence.

254. Non-Christians, by God's gracious initiative, when they are faithful to their own consciences, can live "justified by the grace of God",[199] and thus be "associated to the paschal mystery of Jesus Christ".[200] But due to the sacramental dimension of sanctifying grace, God's working in them tends to produce signs and rites, sacred expressions which in turn bring others to a communitarian experience of journeying towards God.[201] While these lack the meaning and efficacy of the sacraments instituted by Christ, they can be channels which the Holy Spirit raises up in order to liberate non-Christians from atheistic immanentism or from purely individual religious experiences. The same Spirit everywhere brings forth various forms of practical wisdom which help people to bear suffering and to live in greater peace and harmony. As Christians, we can also benefit from these treasures built up over many centuries, which can help us better to live our own beliefs.

Social Dialogue in a Context of Religious Freedom

255. The Synod Fathers spoke of the importance of respect for religious freedom, viewed as a fundamental human

---

199. International Theological Commission, *Christianity and the World Religions* (1996), 72: *Enchiridion Vaticanum* 15, No. 1061.

200. Ibid.

201. Cf. ibid., 81-87: *Enchiridion Vaticanum* 15, Nos. 1070-1076.

right.[202] This includes "the freedom to choose the religion which one judges to be true and to manifest one's beliefs in public".[203] A healthy pluralism, one which genuinely respects differences and values them as such, does not entail privatizing religions in an attempt to reduce them to the quiet obscurity of the individual's conscience or to relegate them to the enclosed precincts of churches, synagogues or mosques. This would represent, in effect, a new form of discrimination and authoritarianism. The respect due to the agnostic or non-believing minority should not be arbitrarily imposed in a way that silences the convictions of the believing majority or ignores the wealth of religious traditions. In the long run, this would feed resentment rather than tolerance and peace.

256. When considering the effect of religion on public life, one must distinguish the different ways in which it is practiced. Intellectuals and serious journalists frequently descend to crude and superficial generalizations in speaking of the shortcomings of religion, and often prove incapable of realizing that not all believers – or religious leaders – are the same. Some politicians take advantage of this confusion to justify acts of discrimination. At other times, contempt is shown for writings which reflect religious convictions, overlooking the fact that religious classics can prove

---

202. Cf. *Propositio* 16.

203. Benedict XVI, Post-Synodal Apostolic Exhortation *Ecclesia in Medio Oriente* (14 September 2012), 26: AAS 104 (2012), 762.

meaningful in every age; they have an enduring power to open new horizons, to stimulate thought, to expand the mind and the heart. This contempt is due to the myopia of a certain rationalism. Is it reasonable and enlightened to dismiss certain writings simply because they arose in a context of religious belief? These writings include principles which are profoundly humanistic and, albeit tinged with religious symbols and teachings, they have a certain value for reason.

257. As believers, we also feel close to those who do not consider themselves part of any religious tradition, yet sincerely seek the truth, goodness and beauty which we believe have their highest expression and source in God. We consider them as precious allies in the commitment to defending human dignity, in building peaceful coexistence between peoples and in protecting creation. A special place of encounter is offered by new Areopagi such as the Court of the Gentiles, where "believers and non-believers are able to engage in dialogue about fundamental issues of ethics, art and science, and about the search for transcendence".[204] This too is a path to peace in our troubled world.

258. Starting from certain social issues of great importance for the future of humanity, I have tried to make explicit once again the inescapable social dimension of the Gospel message and to encourage all Christians to demonstrate it by their words, attitudes and deeds.

---

204. Cf. *Propositio* 55.

CHAPTER FIVE

SPIRIT-FILLED EVANGELIZERS

259. Spirit-filled evangelizers means evangelizers fearlessly open to the working of the Holy Spirit. At Pentecost, the Spirit made the apostles go forth from themselves and turned them into heralds of God's wondrous deeds, capable of speaking to each person in his or her own language. The Holy Spirit also grants the courage to proclaim the newness of the Gospel with boldness (parrhesía) in every time and place, even when it meets with opposition. Let us call upon him today, firmly rooted in prayer, for without prayer all our activity risks being fruitless and our message empty. Jesus wants evangelizers who proclaim the good news not only with words, but above all by a life transfigured by God's presence.

260. In this final chapter, I do not intend to offer a synthesis of Christian spirituality, or to explore great themes like prayer, Eucharistic adoration or the liturgical celebration

of the faith. For all these we already have valuable texts of the magisterium and celebrated writings by great authors. I do not claim to replace or improve upon these treasures. I simply wish to offer some thoughts about the spirit of the new evangelization.

261. Whenever we say that something is "spirited", it usually refers to some interior impulse which encourages, motivates, nourishes and gives meaning to our individual and communal activity. Spirit-filled evangelization is not the same as a set of tasks dutifully carried out despite one's own personal inclinations and wishes. How I long to find the right words to stir up enthusiasm for a new chapter of evangelization full of fervour, joy, generosity, courage, boundless love and attraction! Yet I realize that no words of encouragement will be enough unless the fire of the Holy Spirit burns in our hearts. A spirit-filled evangelization is one guided by the Holy Spirit, for he is the soul of the Church called to proclaim the Gospel. Before offering some spiritual motivations and suggestions, I once more invoke the Holy Spirit. I implore him to come and renew the Church, to stir and impel her to go forth boldly to evangelize all peoples.

I. REASONS FOR A RENEWED MISSIONARY IMPULSE

262. Spirit-filled evangelizers are evangelizers who pray and work. Mystical notions without a solid social and mis-

sionary outreach are of no help to evangelization, nor are dissertations or social or pastoral practices which lack a spirituality which can change hearts. These unilateral and incomplete proposals only reach a few groups and prove incapable of radiating beyond them because they curtail the Gospel. What is needed is the ability to cultivate an interior space which can give a Christian meaning to commitment and activity.[205] Without prolonged moments of adoration, of prayerful encounter with the word, of sincere conversation with the Lord, our work easily becomes meaningless; we lose energy as a result of weariness and difficulties, and our fervour dies out. The Church urgently needs the deep breath of prayer, and to my great joy groups devoted to prayer and intercession, the prayerful reading of God's word and the perpetual adoration of the Eucharist are growing at every level of ecclesial life. Even so, "we must reject the temptation to offer a privatized and individualistic spirituality which ill accords with the demands of charity, to say nothing of the implications of the incarnation".[206] There is always the risk that some moments of prayer can become an excuse for not offering one's life in mission; a privatized lifestyle can lead Christians to take refuge in some false forms of spirituality.

---

205. Cf. *Propositio* 36.

206. John Paul II, Apostolic Letter *Novo Millennio Ineunte* (6 January 2001), 52: AAS 93 (2001), 304.

263. We do well to keep in mind the early Christians and our many brothers and sisters throughout history who were filled with joy, unflagging courage and zeal in proclaiming the Gospel. Some people nowadays console themselves by saying that things are not as easy as they used to be, yet we know that the Roman empire was not conducive to the Gospel message, the struggle for justice, or the defence of human dignity. Every period of history is marked by the presence of human weakness, self-absorption, complacency and selfishness, to say nothing of the concupiscence which preys upon us all. These things are ever present under one guise or another; they are due to our human limits rather than particular situations. Let us not say, then, that things are harder today; they are simply different. But let us learn also from the saints who have gone before us, who confronted the difficulties of their own day. So I propose that we pause to rediscover some of the reasons which can help us to imitate them today.[207]

Personal Encounter with the Saving Love of Jesus

264. The primary reason for evangelizing is the love of Jesus which we have received, the experience of salvation which urges us to ever greater love of him. What kind of love would not feel the need to speak of the beloved, to point him out, to make him known? If we do not feel an

---

207. Cf. V.M. Fernández, "Espiritualidad para la esperanza activa. Discurso en la apertura del I Congreso Nacional de Doctrina Social de la Iglesia (Rosario 2011)", in *UCActualidad*, 142 (2011), 16.

intense desire to share this love, we need to pray insistently that he will once more touch our hearts. We need to implore his grace daily, asking him to open our cold hearts and shake up our lukewarm and superficial existence. Standing before him with open hearts, letting him look at us, we see that gaze of love which Nathaniel glimpsed on the day when Jesus said to him: "I saw you under the fig tree" (Jn 1:48). How good it is to stand before a crucifix, or on our knees before the Blessed Sacrament, and simply to be in his presence! How much good it does us when he once more touches our lives and impels us to share his new life! What then happens is that "we speak of what we have seen and heard" (1 Jn 1:3). The best incentive for sharing the Gospel comes from contemplating it with love, lingering over its pages and reading it with the heart. If we approach it in this way, its beauty will amaze and constantly excite us. But if this is to come about, we need to recover a contemplative spirit which can help us to realize ever anew that we have been entrusted with a treasure which makes us more human and helps us to lead a new life. There is nothing more precious which we can give to others.

265. Jesus' whole life, his way of dealing with the poor, his actions, his integrity, his simple daily acts of generosity, and finally his complete self-giving, is precious and reveals the mystery of his divine life. Whenever we encounter this anew, we become convinced that it is exactly what others need, even though they may not recognize it: "What therefore you worship as unknown, this I proclaim to you"

(Acts 17:23). Sometimes we lose our enthusiasm for mission because we forget that the Gospel responds to our deepest needs, since we were created for what the Gospel offers us: friendship with Jesus and love of our brothers and sisters. If we succeed in expressing adequately and with beauty the essential content of the Gospel, surely this message will speak to the deepest yearnings of people's hearts: "The missionary is convinced that, through the working of the Spirit, there already exists in individuals and peoples an expectation, even if an unconscious one, of knowing the truth about God, about man, and about how we are to be set free from sin and death. The missionary's enthusiasm in proclaiming Christ comes from the conviction that he is responding to that expectation".[208] Enthusiasm for evangelization is based on this conviction. We have a treasure of life and love which cannot deceive, and a message which cannot mislead or disappoint. It penetrates to the depths of our hearts, sustaining and ennobling us. It is a truth which is never out of date because it reaches that part of us which nothing else can reach. Our infinite sadness can only be cured by an infinite love.

266. But this conviction has to be sustained by our own constantly renewed experience of savouring Christ's friendship and his message. It is impossible to persevere in a fervent evangelization unless we are convinced from

---

208. John Paul II, Encyclical Letter *Redemptoris Missio* (7 December 1990), 45: AAS 83 (1991), 292.

personal experience that it is not the same thing to have known Jesus as not to have known him, not the same thing to walk with him as to walk blindly, not the same thing to hear his word as not to know it, and not the same thing to contemplate him, to worship him, to find our peace in him, as not to. It is not the same thing to try to build the world with his Gospel as to try to do so by our own lights. We know well that with Jesus life becomes richer and that with him it is easier to find meaning in everything. This is why we evangelize. A true missionary, who never ceases to be a disciple, knows that Jesus walks with him, speaks to him, breathes with him, works with him. He senses Jesus alive with him in the midst of the missionary enterprise. Unless we see him present at the heart of our missionary commitment, our enthusiasm soon wanes and we are no longer sure of what it is that we are handing on; we lack vigour and passion. A person who is not convinced, enthusiastic, certain and in love, will convince nobody.

267. In union with Jesus, we seek what he seeks and we love what he loves. In the end, what we are seeking is the glory of the Father; we live and act "for the praise of his glorious grace" (Eph 1:6). If we wish to commit ourselves fully and perseveringly, we need to leave behind every other motivation. This is our definitive, deepest and greatest motivation, the ultimate reason and meaning behind all we do: the glory of the Father which Jesus sought at every moment of his life. As the Son, he rejoices eternally to be "close to the Father's heart" (Jn 1:18). If we are missionar-

ies, it is primarily because Jesus told us that "by this my Father is glorified, that you bear much fruit" (Jn 15:8). Beyond all our own preferences and interests, our knowledge and motivations, we evangelize for the greater glory of the Father who loves us.

The Spiritual Savour of Being a People

268. The word of God also invites us to recognise that we are a people: "Once you were no people but now you are God's people" (1 Pet 2:10). To be evangelizers of souls, we need to develop a spiritual taste for being close to people's lives and to discover that this is itself a source of greater joy. Mission is at once a passion for Jesus and a passion for his people. When we stand before Jesus crucified, we see the depth of his love which exalts and sustains us, but at the same time, unless we are blind, we begin to realize that Jesus' gaze, burning with love, expands to embrace all his people. We realize once more that he wants to make use of us to draw closer to his beloved people. He takes us from the midst of his people and he sends us to his people; without this sense of belonging we cannot understand our deepest identity.

269. Jesus himself is the model of this method of evangelization which brings us to the very heart of his people. How good it is for us to contemplate the closeness which he shows to everyone! If he speaks to someone, he looks into their eyes with deep love and concern: "Jesus, looking

upon him, loved him" (Mk 10:21). We see how accessible he is, as he draws near the blind man (cf. Mk 10:46-52) and eats and drinks with sinners (cf. Mk 2:16) without worrying about being thought a glutton and a drunkard himself (cf. Mt 11:19). We see his sensitivity in allowing a sinful woman to anoint his feet (cf. Lk 7:36-50) and in receiving Nicodemus by night (cf. Jn 3:1-15). Jesus' sacrifice on the cross is nothing else than the culmination of the way he lived his entire life. Moved by his example, we want to enter fully into the fabric of society, sharing the lives of all, listening to their concerns, helping them materially and spiritually in their needs, rejoicing with those who rejoice, weeping with those who weep; arm in arm with others, we are committed to building a new world. But we do so not from a sense of obligation, not as a burdensome duty, but as the result of a personal decision which brings us joy and gives meaning to our lives.

270. Sometimes we are tempted to be that kind of Christian who keeps the Lord's wounds at arm's length. Yet Jesus wants us to touch human misery, to touch the suffering flesh of others. He hopes that we will stop looking for those personal or communal niches which shelter us from the maelstrom of human misfortune and instead enter into the reality of other people's lives and know the power of tenderness. Whenever we do so, our lives become wonderfully complicated and we experience intensely what it is to be a people, to be part of a people.

271. It is true that in our dealings with the world, we are told to give reasons for our hope, but not as an enemy who critiques and condemns. We are told quite clearly: "do so with gentleness and reverence" (1 Pet 3:15) and "if possible, so far as it depends upon you, live peaceably with all" (Rom 12:18). We are also told to overcome "evil with good" (Rom 12:21) and to "work for the good of all" (Gal 6:10). Far from trying to appear better than others, we should "in humility count others better" than ourselves (Phil 2:3). The Lord's apostles themselves enjoyed "favour with all the people" (Acts 2:47; 4:21, 33; 5:13). Clearly Jesus does not want us to be grandees who look down upon others, but men and women of the people. This is not an idea of the Pope, or one pastoral option among others; they are injunctions contained in the word of God which are so clear, direct and convincing that they need no interpretations which might diminish their power to challenge us. Let us live them *sine glossa*, without commentaries. By so doing we will know the missionary joy of sharing life with God's faithful people as we strive to light a fire in the heart of the world.

272. Loving others is a spiritual force drawing us to union with God; indeed, one who does not love others "walks in the darkness" (1 Jn 2:11), "remains in death" (1 Jn 3:14) and "does not know God" (1 Jn 4:8). Benedict XVI has said that "closing our eyes to our neighbour also blinds

us to God",[209] and that love is, in the end, the only light which "can always illuminate a world grown dim and give us the courage needed to keep living and working".[210] When we live out a spirituality of drawing nearer to others and seeking their welfare, our hearts are opened wide to the Lord's greatest and most beautiful gifts. Whenever we encounter another person in love, we learn something new about God. Whenever our eyes are opened to acknowledge the other, we grow in the light of faith and knowledge of God. If we want to advance in the spiritual life, then, we must constantly be missionaries. The work of evangelization enriches the mind and the heart; it opens up spiritual horizons; it makes us more and more sensitive to the workings of the Holy Spirit, and it takes us beyond our limited spiritual constructs. A committed missionary knows the joy of being a spring which spills over and refreshes others. Only the person who feels happiness in seeking the good of others, in desiring their happiness, can be a missionary. This openness of the heart is a source of joy, since "it is more blessed to give than to receive" (Acts 20:35). We do not live better when we flee, hide, refuse to share, stop giving and lock ourselves up in own comforts. Such a life is nothing less than slow suicide.

---

209. Benedict XVI, Encyclical Letter, *Deus Caritas Est* (25 December 2005), 16: AAS 98 (2006), 230.

210. Ibid., 39: AAS 98 (2006), 250.

273. My mission of being in the heart of the people is not just a part of my life or a badge I can take off; it is not an "extra" or just another moment in life. Instead, it is something I cannot uproot from my being without destroying my very self. I am a mission on this earth; that is the reason why I am here in this world. We have to regard ourselves as sealed, even branded, by this mission of bringing light, blessing, enlivening, raising up, healing and freeing. All around us we begin to see nurses with soul, teachers with soul, politicians with soul, people who have chosen deep down to be with others and for others. But once we separate our work from our private lives, everything turns grey and we will always be seeking recognition or asserting our needs. We stop being a people.

274. If we are to share our lives with others and generously give of ourselves, we also have to realize that every person is worthy of our giving. Not for their physical appearance, their abilities, their language, their way of thinking, or for any satisfaction that we might receive, but rather because they are God's handiwork, his creation. God created that person in his image, and he or she reflects something of God's glory. Every human being is the object of God's infinite tenderness, and he himself is present in their lives. Jesus offered his precious blood on the cross for that person. Appearances notwithstanding, every person is immensely holy and deserves our love. Consequently, if I can help at least one person to have a better life, that already justifies the offering of my life. It is a wonderful thing to be God's

faithful people. We achieve fulfilment when we break down walls and our heart is filled with faces and names!

The Mysterious Working of the Risen Christ and his Spirit

275. In the second chapter, we reflected on that lack of deep spirituality which turns into pessimism, fatalism, and mistrust. Some people do not commit themselves to mission because they think that nothing will change and that it is useless to make the effort. They think: "Why should I deny myself my comforts and pleasures if I won't see any significant result?" This attitude makes it impossible to be a missionary. It is only a malicious excuse for remaining caught up in comfort, laziness, vague dissatisfaction and empty selfishness. It is a self-destructive attitude, for "man cannot live without hope: life would become meaningless and unbearable".[211] If we think that things are not going to change, we need to recall that Jesus Christ has triumphed over sin and death and is now almighty. Jesus Christ truly lives. Put another way, " if Christ has not been raised, then our preaching is in vain" (1 Cor 15:14). The Gospel tells us that when the first disciples went forth to preach, "the Lord worked with them and confirmed the message" (Mk 16:20). The same thing happens today. We are invited to discover this, to experience it. Christ, risen and glorified,

---

211. Second Special Assembly for Europe of the Synod of Bishops, Final Message, 1: *L'Osservatore Romano*, Weekly English-language edition, 27 October 1999, 5.

is the wellspring of our hope, and he will not deprive us of the help we need to carry out the mission which he has entrusted to us.

276. Christ's resurrection is not an event of the past; it contains a vital power which has permeated this world. Where all seems to be dead, signs of the resurrection suddenly spring up. It is an irresistible force. Often it seems that God does not exist: all around us we see persistent injustice, evil, indifference and cruelty. But it is also true that in the midst of darkness something new always springs to life and sooner or later produces fruit. On razed land life breaks through, stubbornly yet invincibly. However dark things are, goodness always re-emerges and spreads. Each day in our world beauty is born anew, it rises transformed through the storms of history. Values always tend to reappear under new guises, and human beings have arisen time after time from situations that seemed doomed. Such is the power of the resurrection, and all who evangelize are instruments of that power.

277. At the same time, new difficulties are constantly surfacing: experiences of failure and the human weaknesses which bring so much pain. We all know from experience that sometimes a task does not bring the satisfaction we seek, results are few and changes are slow, and we are tempted to grow weary. Yet lowering our arms momentarily out of weariness is not the same as lowering them for good, overcome by chronic discontent and by a listlessness that parches the soul. It also happens that our hearts can

tire of the struggle because in the end we are caught up in ourselves, in a careerism which thirsts for recognition, applause, rewards and status. In this case we do not lower our arms, but we no longer grasp what we seek, the resurrection is not there. In cases like these, the Gospel, the most beautiful message that this world can offer, is buried under a pile of excuses.

278. Faith also means believing in God, believing that he truly loves us, that he is alive, that he is mysteriously capable of intervening, that he does not abandon us and that he brings good out of evil by his power and his infinite creativity. It means believing that he marches triumphantly in history with those who "are called and chosen and faithful" (Rev 17:14). Let us believe the Gospel when it tells us that the kingdom of God is already present in this world and is growing, here and there, and in different ways: like the small seed which grows into a great tree (cf. Mt 13:31-32), like the measure of leaven that makes the dough rise (cf. Mt 13:33) and like the good seed that grows amid the weeds (cf. Mt 13, 24-30) and can always pleasantly surprise us. The kingdom is here, it returns, it struggles to flourish anew. Christ's resurrection everywhere calls forth seeds of that new world; even if they are cut back, they grow again, for the resurrection is already secretly woven into the fabric of this history, for Jesus did not rise in vain. May we never remain on the sidelines of this march of living hope!

279. Because we do not always see these seeds growing, we need an interior certainty, a conviction that God is able to act in every situation, even amid apparent setbacks: "We have this treasure in earthen vessels" (2 Cor 4:7). This certainty is often called "a sense of mystery". It involves knowing with certitude that all those who entrust themselves to God in love will bear good fruit (cf. Jn 15:5). This fruitfulness is often invisible, elusive and unquantifiable. We can know quite well that our lives will be fruitful, without claiming to know how, or where, or when. We may be sure that none of our acts of love will be lost, nor any of our acts of sincere concern for others. No single act of love for God will be lost, no generous effort is meaningless, no painful endurance is wasted. All of these encircle our world like a vital force. Sometimes it seems that our work is fruitless, but mission is not like a business transaction or investment, or even a humanitarian activity. It is not a show where we count how many people come as a result of our publicity; it is something much deeper, which escapes all measurement. It may be that the Lord uses our sacrifices to shower blessings in another part of the world which we will never visit. The Holy Spirit works as he wills, when he wills and where he wills; we entrust ourselves without pretending to see striking results. We know only that our commitment is necessary. Let us learn to rest in the tenderness of the arms of the Father amid our creative and generous commitment. Let us keep marching forward; let us give him everything, allowing him to make our efforts bear fruit in his good time.

280. Keeping our missionary fervour alive calls for firm trust in the Holy Spirit, for it is he who "helps us in our weakness" (Rom 8:26). But this generous trust has to be nourished, and so we need to invoke the Spirit constantly. He can heal whatever causes us to flag in the missionary endeavour. It is true that this trust in the unseen can cause us to feel disoriented: it is like being plunged into the deep and not knowing what we will find. I myself have frequently experienced this. Yet there is no greater freedom than that of allowing oneself to be guided by the Holy Spirit, renouncing the attempt to plan and control everything to the last detail, and instead letting him enlighten, guide and direct us, leading us wherever he wills. The Holy Spirit knows well what is needed in every time and place. This is what it means to be mysteriously fruitful!

The Missionary Power of Intercessory Prayer

281. One form of prayer moves us particularly to take up the task of evangelization and to seek the good of others: it is the prayer of intercession. Let us peer for a moment into the heart of Saint Paul, to see what his prayer was like. It was full of people: "…I constantly pray with you in every one of my prayers for all of you… because I hold you in my heart" (Phil 1:4, 7). Here we see that intercessory prayer does not divert us from true contemplation, since authentic contemplation always has a place for others.

282. This attitude becomes a prayer of gratitude to God for others. "First, I thank my God through Jesus Christ for all of you" (Rom 1:8). It is constant thankfulness: "I give thanks to God always for you because of the grace of God which was given you in Christ Jesus" (1 Cor 1:4); "I thank my God in all my remembrance of you" (Phil 1:3). Far from being suspicious, negative and despairing, it is a spiritual gaze born of deep faith which acknowledges what God is doing in the lives of others. At the same time, it is the gratitude which flows from a heart attentive to others. When evangelizers rise from prayer, their hearts are more open; freed of self-absorption, they are desirous of doing good and sharing their lives with others.

283. The great men and women of God were great intercessors. Intercession is like a "leaven" in the heart of the Trinity. It is a way of penetrating the Father's heart and discovering new dimensions which can shed light on concrete situations and change them. We can say that God's heart is touched by our intercession, yet in reality he is always there first. What our intercession achieves is that his power, his love and his faithfulness are shown ever more clearly in the midst of the people.

II. MARY, MOTHER OF EVANGELIZATION

284. With the Holy Spirit, Mary is always present in the midst of the people. She joined the disciples in praying for

the coming of the Holy Spirit (Acts 1:14) and thus made possible the missionary outburst which took place at Pentecost. She is the Mother of the Church which evangelizes, and without her we could never truly understand the spirit of the new evangelization.

Jesus' Gift to his People

285. On the cross, when Jesus endured in his own flesh the dramatic encounter of the sin of the world and God's mercy, he could feel at his feet the consoling presence of his mother and his friend. At that crucial moment, before fully accomplishing the work which his Father had entrusted to him, Jesus said to Mary: "Woman, here is your son". Then he said to his beloved friend: "Here is your mother" (Jn 19:26-27). These words of the dying Jesus are not chiefly the expression of his devotion and concern for his mother; rather, they are a revelatory formula which manifests the mystery of a special saving mission. Jesus left us his mother to be our mother. Only after doing so did Jesus know that "all was now finished" (Jn 19:28). At the foot of the cross, at the supreme hour of the new creation, Christ led us to Mary. He brought us to her because he did not want us to journey without a mother, and our people read in this maternal image all the mysteries of the Gospel. The Lord did not want to leave the Church without this icon of womanhood. Mary, who brought him into the world with great faith, also accompanies "the rest of her offspring, those who keep the commandments of God

and bear testimony to Jesus" (Rev 12:17). The close connection between Mary, the Church and each member of the faithful, based on the fact that each in his or her own way brings forth Christ, has been beautifully expressed by Blessed Isaac of Stella: "In the inspired Scriptures, what is said in a universal sense of the virgin mother, the Church, is understood in an individual sense of the Virgin Mary... In a way, every Christian is also believed to be a bride of God's word, a mother of Christ, his daughter and sister, at once virginal and fruitful... Christ dwelt for nine months in the tabernacle of Mary's womb. He dwells until the end of the ages in the tabernacle of the Church's faith. He will dwell forever in the knowledge and love of each faithful soul".[212]

286. Mary was able to turn a stable into a home for Jesus, with poor swaddling clothes and an abundance of love. She is the handmaid of the Father who sings his praises. She is the friend who is ever concerned that wine not be lacking in our lives. She is the woman whose heart was pierced by a sword and who understands all our pain. As mother of all, she is a sign of hope for peoples suffering the birth pangs of justice. She is the missionary who draws near to us and accompanies us throughout life, opening our hearts to faith by her maternal love. As a true mother, she walks at our side, she shares our struggles and she constantly surrounds us with God's love. Through her many titles, of-

---

212. Isaac of Stella, *Sermo* 51: PL 194, 1863, 1865.

ten linked to her shrines, Mary shares the history of each people which has received the Gospel and she becomes a part of their historic identity. Many Christian parents ask that their children be baptized in a Marian shrine, as a sign of their faith in her motherhood which brings forth new children for God. There, in these many shrines, we can see how Mary brings together her children who with great effort come as pilgrims to see her and to be seen by her. Here they find strength from God to bear the weariness and the suffering in their lives. As she did with Juan Diego, Mary offers them maternal comfort and love, and whispers in their ear: "Let your heart not be troubled... Am I not here, who am your Mother?"[213]

Star of the New Evangelization

287. We ask the Mother of the living Gospel to intercede that this invitation to a new phase of evangelization will be accepted by the entire ecclesial community. Mary is the woman of faith, who lives and advances in faith,[214] and "her exceptional pilgrimage of faith represents a constant point of reference for the Church".[215] Mary let herself be guided by the Holy Spirit on a journey of faith towards a destiny of service and fruitfulness. Today we look to her

---

213. *Nican Mopohua*, 118-119.

214. Cf. Second Vatican Ecumenical Council, Dogmatic Constitution on the Church *Lumen Gentium*, 52-69.

215. John Paul II, Encyclical Letter *Redemptoris Mater* (25 March 1987), 6: AAS 79 (1987), 366-367.

and ask her to help us proclaim the message of salvation to all and to enable new disciples to become evangelizers in turn.[216] Along this journey of evangelization we will have our moments of aridity, darkness and even fatigue. Mary herself experienced these things during the years of Jesus' childhood in Nazareth: "This is the beginning of the Gospel, the joyful good news. However, it is not difficult to see in that beginning a particular heaviness of heart, linked with a sort of night of faith – to use the words of Saint John of the Cross – a kind of 'veil' through which one has to draw near to the Invisible One and to live in intimacy with the mystery. And this is the way that Mary, for many years, lived in intimacy with the mystery of her Son, and went forward in her pilgrimage of faith".[217]

288. There is a Marian "style" to the Church's work of evangelization. Whenever we look to Mary, we come to believe once again in the revolutionary nature of love and tenderness. In her we see that humility and tenderness are not virtues of the weak but of the strong who need not treat others poorly in order to feel important themselves. Contemplating Mary, we realize that she who praised God for "bringing down the mighty from their thrones" and "sending the rich away empty" (Lk 1:52-53) is also the one who brings a homely warmth to our pursuit of justice.

---

216. Cf. *Propositio* 58.

217. John Paul II, Encyclical Letter *Redemptoris Mater* (25 March 1987), 17: AAS 79 (1987), 381.

She is also the one who carefully keeps "all these things, pondering them in her heart" (Lk 2:19). Mary is able to recognize the traces of God's Spirit in events great and small. She constantly contemplates the mystery of God in our world, in human history and in our daily lives. She is the woman of prayer and work in Nazareth, and she is also Our Lady of Help, who sets out from her town "with haste" (Lk 1:39) to be of service to others. This interplay of justice and tenderness, of contemplation and concern for others, is what makes the ecclesial community look to Mary as a model of evangelization. We implore her maternal intercession that the Church may become a home for many peoples, a mother for all peoples, and that the way may be opened to the birth of a new world. It is the Risen Christ who tells us, with a power that fills us with confidence and unshakeable hope: "Behold, I make all things new" (Rev 21:5). With Mary we advance confidently towards the fulfilment of this promise, and to her we pray:

Mary, Virgin and Mother,
you who, moved by the Holy Spirit,
welcomed the word of life
in the depths of your humble faith:
as you gave yourself completely to the Eternal One,
help us to say our own "yes"
to the urgent call, as pressing as ever,
to proclaim the good news of Jesus.

Filled with Christ's presence,
you brought joy to John the Baptist,

making him exult in the womb of his mother.
Brimming over with joy,
you sang of the great things done by God.
Standing at the foot of the cross
with unyielding faith,
you received the joyful comfort of the resurrection,
and joined the disciples in awaiting the Spirit
so that the evangelizing Church might be born.

Obtain for us now a new ardour born of the resurrection,
that we may bring to all the Gospel of life
which triumphs over death.
Give us a holy courage to seek new paths,
that the gift of unfading beauty
may reach every man and woman.

Virgin of listening and contemplation,
Mother of love, Bride of the eternal wedding feast,
pray for the Church, whose pure icon you are,
that she may never be closed in on herself
or lose her passion for establishing God's kingdom.

Star of the new evangelization,
help us to bear radiant witness to communion,
service, ardent and generous faith,
justice and love of the poor,
that the joy of the Gospel
may reach to the ends of the earth,
illuminating even the fringes of our world.

Mother of the living Gospel,
wellspring of happiness for God's little ones,
pray for us.
Amen. Alleluia!

Given in Rome, at Saint Peter's, on 24 November, the solemnity of Our Lord Jesus Christ, King of the Universe, and the conclusion of the Year of Faith, in the year 2013, the first of my Pontificate.

Franciscus

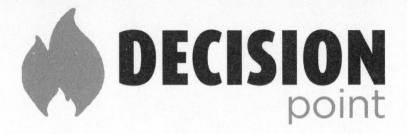

NOTES

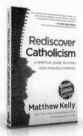

NOTES

NOTES

NOTES

NOTES

NOTES

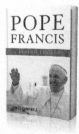

Pope Francis: A Living Legacy
James Campbell

NOTES

NOTES